THE SPIES AT GILNAHIRK

- ..../ ... --. .. ..../.- -/ --. .. .-.. -. .- .... -. -.-

GEORGE BUSBY

BALLYHAY BOOKS

Published by Ballyhay Books,
an imprint of Laurel Cottage Ltd.,
Donaghadee, Northern Ireland.
Copyrights reserved.
© George Busby 2016.
Photographs are reproduced by permission.
All rights reserved.
No part of this book may be reproduced or stored on any media
without the express written permission of the publishers.
Printed by Gutenberg Press, Malta.
ISBN 978-1-910657-08-9

A WORD OF THANKS

Since 2004 I have been amazed how helpful people have been during my quest to uncover the history and purpose of Gilnahirk Wireless Station. There are so many I need to thank and while space prevents me mentioning them all here, there are some who I simply must acknowledge.

William Gilpin the young man from Regent House Grammar School who triggered my interest; Bob King and Stan Ames, two English gentlemen who kept me on the straight and narrow and supplied a great deal of material relating directly to Gilnahirk from Kew in London and other mainland locations; Ray Wright from New Zealand, who was at Gilnahirk in 1945 and sent material and photographs from New Zealand; Tony Banham father of the officer in charge at Gilnahirk who supplied much vital material; Pamela Allen, daughter of the first Voluntary Interceptor I discovered in Northern Ireland, for sharing her father's memories and radio log sheets with me; George Browne who allowed me to share and reproduce a great deal of the material belonging to his late friend Mr Arthur Irwin (GI5TK) of Ballygowan; the families of William Kerr, Stanley Johnston, Jack Smyth, Desmond Downing, Steve Dorman, Albert Wright, Joshua Bell, Edgar Byrnes and Joe Parke for sharing memories, and material from that period in our local history. What a difference it makes when you have material with firm links to the Northern Ireland operation.

In addition to these individuals there were a number of organisations and groups whose help was invaluable and my thanks are due to all the staff of the Somme Heritage Centre who gave my research a well needed boost in its earliest days, in particular Richard Parkinson and Bob McKinley's help in putting together a Power Point presentation and lecture I could deliver to various groups and to all those who invited me to speak to those groups across the province, for it was through your invitations that I was then able to discover the names of some of our Voluntary Interceptors in Northern Ireland. Thanks also to the Amateur Radio Fraternity for their assistance in understanding the world of amateur radio and its problems and to the late Pat Hawker, Angus Annan and in particular to Brian Moore who kindly restored and donated a working HRO receiver which some day in the future will become part of a display at the Somme Heritage Centre publicising the work of the RSS and our VIs. Also his good friend Roy McKinty.

Finally, I wish to thank Mr Eric Minnis for putting up with me when he was redeveloping the Gilnahirk site and for his assistance in getting the former WWII site named plus plaques erected. To my publishers Ballyhay Books for making this book possible and last but by no means least my good wife Joan for her patience and understanding during twelve years of what she must have considered at times absolute madness.

CONTENTS

The Gilnahirk wireless station in 1968

For many years the people who worked at or were associated with the unpretentious group of buildings nestling quietly in the Castlereagh Hills at Gilnahirk were more than happy that their activities went unremarked by the general population, few realising what the site was and even fewer knowing what went on there.

Quietly listening to and gathering data on the radio transmissions of Britain's enemies both active and potential, the organisation based at Gilnahirk preferred to remain in the shadows even long after it had formally closed its doors in 1978.

7

Bletchley Park

However, few things remain secret forever and by the mid 1970s books such as Wing Commander F.W. Winterbotham's *The Ultra Secret* had begun to raise the veil of secrecy which, for many years, had been drawn tightly around the story of the war effort of Britain's intelligence services although even today many key elements of the story remain hidden from the public's view.

In the intervening period much of the spotlight has focussed on the activities of the code breakers based at Bletchley Park and some of its leading lights such as Alan Turing, Gordon Welchman, Tommy Flowers and Ulsterman John Herivel are, if not household names, at least well known in the public domain.

However, while Bletchley Park may have been the jewel in the crown of the British intelligence effort during the war, the attention it receives often disguises the fact that it was only a cog in a much larger machine without which Bletchley Park would have been as much use as a car with no fuel.

As Bletchley Park code breaker Asa Briggs explains in his book *Secret Days*. *"When I moved to BP in the late spring of 1943 there were no fewer than 2,640 civilians and 2,430 service men and women working in BP and its scattered out-stations, all of which belonged to the same complex. We depended on them as much as on the people working in BP."*

Before the mathematical and linguistic wizards of Bletchley Park could apply their unique skills and technology to the task of deciphering the enemy's messages, the raw material had to be gathered in and to do this a vast chain of listeners was required.

Some of this requirement was fulfilled by elements from all three of the armed services who, through bitter experience from the Great War, had learned the value of keeping tabs on the signals traffic of their opposite numbers and had maintained this capability in the inter-

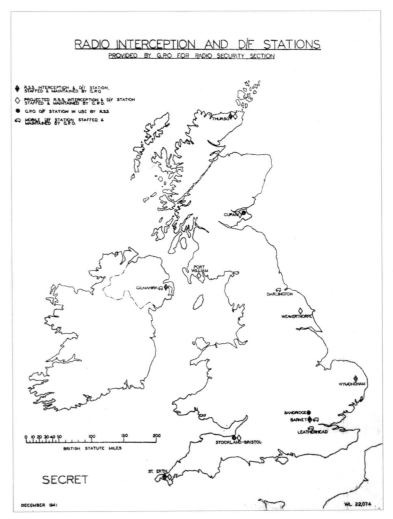

Listening stations operating on behalf of the RSS in 1941

vening period of peace. In addition to these military eavesdropping operations the services of elements of the Foreign Office and the GPO were also added to the mix ensuring that Bletchley Park could rely on a rich seam of intercepted signals on which to ply its trade. These operations were originally known as the 'Wireless Intercept Service'

Mr Bob King at home in his radio shack is the driving force behind the RSS / SCU reunions and the preservation of the contribution made by the Radio Security Service to the work of Bletchley Park during WWII. Without Bob I fear I may not have achieved the success I did. It was he who alerted me to the work of the Voluntary Interceptors

which through the abbreviation to 'WI' service became known as the 'Y' service.

The 'Y' service was primarily an outward looking operation seeking to eavesdrop on signals emanating from Germany and the territories she had occupied, but Britain faced another threat – that of spies located within her own borders – which would require a radio listening service which would look inwards. To this end the Radio Security Section (later to become the Radio Security Service or RSS) was established after a secret War Office meeting at the end of 1938.

The RSS moved quickly to establish a network of listening stations based on the existing GPO network plus three new stations, including one at Gilnahirk, which were soon contributing to the overall war effort. These stations were primarily manned by GPO staff under the direction of officers from the RSS.

In the same way that Bletchley Park could not operate in a vacuum, these new listening stations also drew on outside help. Complementing the high frequency intercept work at these new stations were a specially selected group of radio operators made up of radio amateurs, ex-service, ex-commercial, ex-merchant marine and ex-Air Ministry personnel known simply as Voluntary Interceptors. All of these VIs would work from within their own homes at various locations across the province from as far apart as the village of Clogher in County Tyrone to the town of Portrush on the North Antrim Coast.

However it soon became clear that the spy threat what not as great as originally perceived and the focus of the RSS changed from monitoring the airwaves trying to identify Abwher agents in the UK to monitoring the Abwher signals emanating from bases on continental Europe.

Voluntary Interceptors were each instructed to monitor a specific section of the short wave band for faint signals which did not fit normal patterns of commercial or military traffic. By listening to the same small range of frequencies, the VIs would become accustomed to the regular signals and would therefore be able to pick up on the occasional, faint transmissions which were of interest.

By 1942 Gilnahirk consisted of five buildings (three brick built and two wooden) plus an underground metal cabin. The station had sections which specialised in High Frequency Interception, High Frequency Direction Finding, Medium Frequency Direction Finding as well as a mobile Direction Finding and Intercept unit. By this time Gilnahirk, along with the other RSS stations, had ceased to be a civilian organisation. As their operations had evolved their main mission had changed from hunting for possible spies resident in the UK to monitoring the radio traffic between the various command centres which controlled the German spy networks throughout Europe and beyond. This change of mission made it sensible to place the RSS under the wing of MI6 putting the whole operation on a military footing.

During the War all those involved were sworn to the strictest secrecy for this was all part of the "Ultra" process. To quote Churchill, *"Bletchley Park was the Goose that the laid the Golden Eggs,"* and at the end of WWII the work which had gone on at Bletchley Park was concealed behind the Official Secrets Act. Adding to this cloak of secrecy in May 1945 a strict order, 'action immediately' was issued by the director of military intelligence stating clearly that all documentary evidence of what had taken place at Bletchley Park and the out stations must be destroyed at once leaving no evidence or trace of any kind on site.

There was a blanket ban on all who had been involved to ever say anything about what they had been doing during the war and by the time that strictly imposed silence was gradually removed from 1974 onwards it was too late for many to speak.

In Northern Ireland the majority of those involved had already gone to their grave and taken their secrets and their memories with then.

This was particularly regrettable as the majority of their families and friends knew nothing of the vital part they had played in the Allies victory, their many hours of listening and recording going unrewarded apart from the personal satisfaction derived from having participated in a job well done.

Part of the reason for all this secrecy was that after the War the skills and techniques developed during the war to intercept, analyse and decode the radio transmissions of the enemy were still at the cutting edge and became even more crucial as erstwhile allies became foes. Far from being discarded, the methods of gathering intelligence from radio interceptions were further honed and developed as the Cold War intensified and Gilnahirk was not switched off until 1978 when advances in communications technology made it redundant.

Of course all this secrecy makes researching the history of Gilnahirk a less than straight forward task but in the following pages I've sought to present the results of over a decade of research into the activities of this fascinating and secretive establishment which for so many years quietly listened to and recorded communications considered vital to the security of the UK's citizens.

This publication will for the first time reveal what is known of the contribution made by the Gilnahirk station in Northern Ireland. This is not a name nor a location that one normally associates with the work of Bletchley Park but it can rightly say without fear of contradiction that 'We Also Served'.

Since the dawn of the nation state, gathering information by all means possible on neighbouring countries, their activities and their intentions has been a vital tool in ensuring the state's security. Such means have always included the use of observers in other countries who can report back first hand what is happening. When such observers are on the staff of your embassy they are known as diplomats, those not on embassy staff are known as spies.

WWII High frequency radio in a suitcase – ideal for clandestine communications.

In times of war embassies are closed down and spies become vital in assessing your enemy's capabilities and intentions as well as having the potential to damage their war effort through acts of sabotage.

In earlier conflicts the work of spies was often hampered by the difficulties they faced in receiving instructions from, and getting information back to, their masters. However with advances in wireless communication this hurdle had largely been overcome as the storm clouds of war gathered in the late 1930s. Both in the public mind and in official circles there was considerable concern that the country could be widely infiltrated by spies who would report back on Britain's preparations for war. It was also thought that if hostilities commenced these spies could use radios to guide bombers onto key targets which, given the prevailing wisdom as espoused by Prime Minister Stanley Baldwin in a speech in 1932 that 'the bomber will always get through' was not a happy thought.

The concerns were given considerable authenticity by the Arthur Owens affair in the late 1930s.

13

Arthur Graham Owens was a salesman with a British company which made ships' batteries and in the 1930s was making regular trips from England to Germany where he had gained contracts with the German Navy, the Kreigsmarine. In 1936 Arthur was briefly engaged by MI6 to report on what he had seen and heard during his regular visits to German shipyards. However Arthur had also won contracts to supply the Royal Navy with batteries and during his visits to Europe he was approached by the German intelligence service the Abwehr who, presumably being aware that as an ardent Welsh Nationalist Arthur had little or no loyalty to the United Kingdom, asked him to become a spy for them.

Thankfully MI5 had placed Arthur on a watch list after the Royal Mail had discovered that Arthur was sending mail to a known cover address in Germany used by the Abwehr. It was time to act and further investigations confirmed that Arthur was indeed working as a spy for Germany. On his return from Germany he was arrested and brought before the courts who then placed him into the jurisdiction of British Military Intelligence. Under further integration Arthur revealed the existence of a German spy radio set which British intelligence then recovered from a left luggage locker at a central London railway station. The threat from Germany to the United Kingdom was real and up front.

The nature of the expected threat and a technical analysis of what could be done about it is detailed in *Appendix 1: Illicit Wireless Intercept Organisation General instructions*.

While there were a number of wireless eavesdropping assets already in place seeking to listen in to German radio transmissions, they were fully engaged in their existing duties and for various technical reasons (see appendix 1) were not ideally suited to identifying and tracing illegal radio transmissions originating within the UK.

Given the magnitude of the perceived threat and the lack of available assets to tackle it a secret War Office meeting took place on Tuesday December 13th 1938 to discuss the creation of an organisation within the United Kingdom to detect Illicit Wireless Transmissions as soon as possible. Out of this meeting the Radio Security Section (RSS) was born.

Present at the meeting were nine gentlemen from various backgrounds. Military Intelligence, the Foreign Office and the General Post Office. The chairman Colonel KW Martin DSO brought to the attention of those present a directive from the Committee of Imperial Defence (issued in 1933) that the following would apply in a time of national emergency; *The War Office should be responsible in peace and war for the direction and finance of an organisation for the detection of illicit wireless transmissions. The Post Office to act as agents for the War Office and to provide material and personnel for this purpose.'*

Twenty-four good men were chosen from within the ranks of Royal Signals and Military Intelligence to run the RSS at grass roots level under the command of Colonel Worlledge. Their first headquarters would be in 'C' Wing of Worm Wood Scrubs prison where MI5 had established itself just prior to the outbreak of WWII.

Based on the radio set recovered in the Owens affair, it was believed that the radios which would be used by German spies would broadcast in the shortwave section of the radio spectrum which

Extract from the meeting when the RSS was established

The Officers of the Radio Security Service
Back row left to right, followed
by centre and front row.
Etherdge, Penham ?, Berkley, Lakin,
Vale, Roper, Unknown, Banham.
Lloyd, Bellringer, Tant, Sabine,
Scarratt, Lord Sandhurst, Rolfe, Evans,
Rutland, Watherson, Unknown.
Adams, Stratton, Worlledge, Lacey, Hall.
The Steward is sitting on the ground
and was known as Paddy.
Colonel Worlledge was the officer in
charge from 1938 until December
1941. He was replaced by Morton
Evans in January 1942 and remained
in place until the end of the war.
In later life Hugh Trevor Roper became
Lord Dacre, professor of modern
history at Oxford University.
Bellringer was the recruiting officer a
gentleman who most knew both during
and after the war as the signals intelligence
operation moved into the world of GCHQ.

presented a problem. Due to the way radio waves from this part of the spectrum propagate, to stand a good change of picking up an illicit signal would require a network of listening posts spread across the whole country. As a first step the RSS would also establish a series of nine regional offices across the whole of the United Kingdom in: Thurso and Stirling in Scotland; Belfast in Northern Ireland; Preston, Leicester, Cambridge, Leatherhead and Exeter in England; and a final office would be located in Cardiff, Wales.

The War Office would fund the whole operation but the Post Office would act as agents providing everything from engineering and equipment to manpower. Ultimate control would rest with military intelligence who would oversee what was in effect a civilian operation.

The officer appointed to look after the needs and requirements of the RSS operation in Northern Ireland was Captain Joe Banham and with his appointment the seeds of the Gilnahirk station were planted and ready to germinate.

Northern Ireland was an obvious target for the German Abwehr for a number of reasons besides being strategically important in terms of defending the vital North Atlantic supply routes. Situated at or beyond the maximum range of the Luftwaffe bombers and with the largest shipyard in the world, an aircraft factory and a whole series of heavy engineering plants, Northern Ireland would be a major production centre for the large amounts of the materials which would be required in the event of a war with Germany.

You never know who's on the wires!

BE CAREFUL WHAT YOU SAY

WWII public information poster

Another opportunity for the Abwehr was the makeup of our population. The Irish republican cause contained a small number of extremists within the island of Ireland who, if we went to war with Germany, would doubtless seize on the opportunity of hurting Britain by assisting Germany in any way possible. In the spirit of the proverb 'My enemies' enemy, is my friend.' they would be only too willing to spy for the Abwehr and, given explosives and guns, they would gladly disrupt Britain's war production. If the German Abwehr had recruited a Welsh Nationalist to spy on Britain, the possibility of an Irish Nationalist being involved could not be ignored.

In addition, the proximity of the Republic of Ireland which remained neutral during the war and where the German Legation remained open throughout, posed another threat. During my research I came across the following whilst searching through the records in London. Although it is not a Radio Security Service Interception, it provides evidence of German activity in Eire.

Telephone House, Cromac Street

A German Spy
Winkie Loughran, Wireless Operator, Isle of Islay, Scotland.

I relayed ranges and details of aircraft in code to Castlerock, Northern Ireland from Saligo Bay.

One day, while I was "working" Ireland on our secret frequency I was interrupted by an unknown sender. I managed to keep him sending by telling him in our international Morse," I can't hear well. Keep sending." Meanwhile, our boss of the watch got a station down the coast to try and locate his position. Several days later the station notified us that he had been found and proved to be a German spy with a wireless set out on a point off land of the coast of Ireland!

As such, shortly after the War Office meeting where the RSS was established, plans were put in place to set up an outstation in Northern Ireland to be set up under the command of Captain Joe Banham.

The date of Captain Joe Banham's arrival in Northern Ireland is unknown, but we do know that he established his first regional office within room three of Telephone House, Cromac Street, Belfast. This was the engineering headquarters of the Post Office and would allow Captain Banham to be in a position where he could oversee the day to day construction of the site and, if required, give leverage by way of the War Office if there were any problems.

Reference has been made earlier to a directive from the Committee of Imperial Defence (issued in 1933) that in a time of national emergency;

"The War Office should be responsible in peace and war for the direction and finance of an organisation for the detection of illicit wireless transmissions. The Post Office to act as agents for the War Office and to provide material and personnel for this purpose."

And again Captain Banham setting up office within the GPO indicates their central role in the whole operation. It is probably worthwhile to take a minor diversion from the main thread of our story to explain how the GPO came to be in this position.

The GPO, Masters of Communications

The roots of the GPO date back to the early 16th century when a service was put in place to protect and deliver the King's mail under the auspices of the Master of Posts.

The system developed over the ensuing century until in 1635 the mail system which had been for the exclusive use of the Royal court, was made available to the public under the private control of a Thomas Witherings. Then in 1660 under the reign of Charles the Second, an act of parliament finally established the General Post Office.

WWII public information poster

With the flow of private correspondence across the nation under state control it was only natural that the nation's protectors would use this system to spy when necessary on those they considered a threat to our national security. Over many years the GPO devised various means that would allow anything of suspicion to be opened and read – no matter what means the sender may have gone to in trying to conceal his correspondence – with neither the sender nor the receiver any the wiser.

Although there were alternative ways to send messages such as semaphore, mail was the transmission method of choice until the arrival of the electric telegraph in the 1800s. Initially the networks were owned and built by various private companies, often in parallel with the ever expanding rail network but, by the late 1800s, concerns about private monopolies controlling such a vital national resource led to the British Government nationalising all the countries telegraph companies under terms of the Telegraph Act of 1868. The task of running the newly nationalised company was given to the Post Master General which,

An excellent example of how the ability of the security services to tap into telegraph messages could be used to influence international relations is the story of the Zimmerman Telegram. In 1917 during WW1 a coded diplomatic message from the German Foreign Office to the German Ambassador in Mexico had to be sent via American telegraph lines as the British had dredged up and cut the German transatlantic lines. In a mistake they were to repeat 20-odd years later, the Germans felt the message was safe from prying eyes as it was highly encrypted but the British had tapped into the American line where it surfaced in the UK (to be boosted for its long jump across the Atlantic) and their code breakers were able to extract the message.

We intend to begin on the first of February unrestricted submarine warfare. We shall endeavor in spite of this to keep the United States of America neutral. In the event of this not succeeding, we make Mexico a proposal of alliance on the following basis: make war together, make peace together, generous financial support and an understanding on our part that Mexico is to reconquer the lost territory in Texas, New Mexico, and Arizona. The settlement in detail is left to you. You will inform the President of the above most secretly as soon as the outbreak of war with the United States of America is certain and add the suggestion that he should, on his own initiative, invite Japan to immediate adherence and at the same time mediate between Japan and ourselves. Please call the President's attention to the fact that the ruthless employment of our submarines now offers the prospect of compelling England in a few months to make peace." Signed, ZIMMERMANN

cont over...

given that the electric telegraph was effectively the internet of its day, catapulted the GPO to the forefront of communications technology. More importantly, in terms of our story, this centralisation meant that close co-operation between the security services and the GPO in monitoring suspicious mail was easily extended to this new means of communications.

When wireless telegraphy arrived at the start of the 20th century once again there were initially no restrictions on the use of the new technology but within a few years the British government stepped in to regulate the use of the airwaves within Britain with the passing of Wireless Telegraphy Act of 1904. Once again the natural organisation to licence and police the new rules was the GPO.

A system of licencing was introduced and, if that licence covered the ability to transmit as well as receive, the individual holding the licence had to undergo a period of training and examination in Wireless Telegraphy. This would include a basic understanding of wireless theory; wireless maintenance and, crucially, the individual operator would have to learn Morse code.

Morse code, introduced by Samuel F. B. Morse, a third generation Ulster Scot whose grandparents had emigrated to America from Mullabrack in County Armagh, Northern Ireland, was the almost universal language of wireless telegraphy before and during WW2 for several reasons.

1) In conditions where, due to static interference or a weak signal, a voice transmission would be unintelligible a Morse signal could still be discerned.

2) Transmitters capable of sending Morse code were simpler and required considerably less power than those for voice transmission

3) Messages sent in Morse code could be encrypted either by hand or by machine (such as the Enigma device) prior to transmission making communications much more secure.

These qualifications applied to everyone operating a radio transmitter. If you failed to obtain a licence, or if you failed to comply and obey the laws relating to wireless telegraphy whilst holding a valid licence you were breaking the law.

In Northern Ireland the enforcement of these licenced regulations was conducted from the GPO's Ballygomartin radio station. If a problem arose with a licensed transmitter a letter from the GPO wire-

cont...

Having taken some trouble to disguise the real source of the message, the British passed it to the Americans where it greatly inflamed anti-German sentiment and significantly contributed to the United States entry to the war against Germany – a perfect example of wiretapping at its best.

The GPO's wireless station at Enoch Hill, Ballygomartin. The receiving aerial which consists of eight inverted 'V's is in the foreground

less telegraphy department would have been sent out giving details of the interference, misuse or other cause of concern and it was then up to that licence holder to rectify the problem as quickly as possible.

GPO Detector Van

Failure to comply could result in a withdrawal of licence and the possible confiscation of the radio equipment.

For unlicensed transmissions reported to them or detected by the GPO personnel, a special department within the GPO engineering section known simply as the Illicit Wireless Intercept Organisation, who were equipped with a mobile listening unit, would try to pinpoint the source of the transmission and a warrant to search the location would be obtained through the Royal Ulster Constabulary. A GPO engineer from the IWIO accompanied by an officer of the RUC would then search the location for the offending transmitter and if found, the unlicensed radio operator would then have been brought before the courts under the wireless telegraph act.

Construction of Gilnahirk

As war with Germany was officially declared on Sunday morning the 3rd September 1939 the need for the RSS to move up a gear began with an instruction from the war office to the Postmaster General.

You are to put in place as soon as possible three new wireless (listening / interception) stations. These three stations will work exclusively to the needs and requirements of the RSS.

The three new wireless stations were to be situated at St Erth in Cornwall, Thurso in the far north of Scotland with a third to be located in Northern Ireland to address the Irish Republican threat which was not being under estimated.

Sadly, we have no precise date for this instruction but it would appear that very shortly after the declaration of hostilities the Wireless Telegraphy department of the Post Office in Northern Ireland began surveying possible locations to try and find a single site capable of accommodating all the signals intelligence facilities required by an Illicit Wireless Intercept Organisation.

I have not been able to identify which sites were considered apart from a few anecdotes such as that related by Alan Hill of Braeside nursery, not far from the final Gilnahirk site, who recalls his father telling of a Post Office caravan in which engineers were conducting tests in connection with the quality of local radio reception.

No matter when and where the various surveys were carried out, a suitable site was found in November near the village

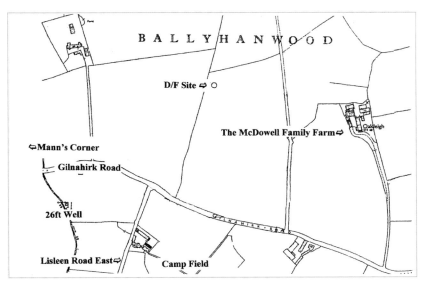

Gilnahirk site

of Gilnahirk, within five miles of Belfast city centre. It had all the attendant advantages of proximity of accommodation for staff and support services. The site on high ground (about 130m or 425ft above sea level) and away from main roads, was almost entirely concealed from general view and its existence has remained virtually unknown to all but a few residents of the local area. Situated in the townland of Ballyhanwood, at the junction of the Gilnahirk and Lisleen Road East the various elements of the wireless station site would be accommodated in three separate fields. On site accommodation for the staff was unnecessary as they all lived in the greater Belfast area. A local bus service operated from Belfast city centre to Mann's Corner and from there it was only a short walk to the site.

Given the powers the government had taken on with the passing of Emergency Powers (Defence) Act 1939 it was not unusual during WWII for new structures to appear out of nowhere with no prior knowledge of the local population but even at that, the construction of the Gilnahirk Wireless Station itself appears to have been conducted

Linking the Gilnahirk site into the much bigger RSS network was once again the responsibility of the GPO. A telephone service had been extended to the site, something no one else had in the surrounding Ballyhanwood area. Special telephone circuits were then provided from Knock telephone exchange at Ballyhackamore with backups from Dundonald and Comber telephone exchanges. These circuits provided constant communications with Gilnahirk from the Barnet Conference Amplifier and the Control Position twenty-four seven.

in what I can only be describe as a very clandestine manner. When interviewing those who could remember the wartime station, most said it appeared as if by magic. There was no mass intrusion by men and machines, things were done in such a way that the construction went largely unnoticed outside the local community.

The late Jim McDowell whose family farm 'Oakleigh' was adjacent to the site recalls the unannounced arrival of a team of Post Office engineers in November 1939. A tented village was soon erected and work began almost immediately. Jim's only real memory of the construction was the continual smell of cooking at various times of the day which lingered over the surrounding area.

Jimmy Mann another close neighbour of the site recalls the erection of many wooden telegraph poles. Never before had he witnessed so many at one location. Jimmy's only other memory of the site was the excavation of a very large hole which, from his description, I believe was to house the underground metal cabin used for the direction finding part of the operation.

Apart from the various buildings on site the provision of utilities like electric, telephone and water had also to be considered. These would all take time to bring to the location. The Gilnahirk facility was to include one Medium Wave Direction Finding Station. One Short Wave Direction Finding Station and a Wireless station with twelve intercept positions. The number of civilian staff is given as fifty-eight.

To physically go and ferret out any illicit wireless broadcasting equipment whose transmissions had been detected, nine mobile vans and six all wave Direction Finding receivers were made available. The number of civilian staff is given as thirty-six.

Up to May 1940 the requirements of the Radio Security Section in Northern Ireland had been provided by the only GPO radio station in the province at Ballygomartin where four listening positions were allocated to the work of the illicit wireless intercept organisation. No precise date had been revealed when Gilnahirk wireless station was switched on, but a single page, hand written RSS document (marked Secret) states that Ballygomartin was switched off in May 1940 although other sources have suggested it was a little later. This possible conflict of dates may be explained by other evidence I have which suggests that the handover did not go as smoothly as planned.

In an interview with the late Robert Martin Armour, a senior member of the management team with the Shorts missile division,

This remarkable photograph of GPO Gilnahirk Wireless Station was taken towards of the end of the war by signalman Alan Sharpe. It is believed to be the only known photograph of the station. Constructed of wood this was a standard bungalow type building provided by the GPO. The length of the building could be shortened or lengthened according to the individual requirement. Despite its position as shown on the previous page the building was actually hidden from the main Gilnahirk road.

A high hedge, plus a field that is dropping away from the road was enough to conceal its presence. From the air the building would have been considered as just another farm building and would not have been seen as out of place in the surrounding countryside.

If we look closely at this document, we have a hand written account of the state of the GPO stations in 1940. May is crossed out. Ballygomartin, N.I. had been providing four positions for the work of the IWIO but according to this note, was closed in May 1940.

The documentation I have seen and read covers only the Post Office aspects of the Gilnahirk site, but I have been made aware that a number of other buildings were constructed of brick at the same time as the rest of the site. This aspect of the station site was known locally as the camp field and contained a small Royal Signals establishment. It is believed that this was a Special Communications Unit of which there were a number throughout the British Isles. Security was extremely tight around these buildings as they contained a very secure means of communications. Constructed with the primary purpose of maintaining a level of command and control for national government during a state of extreme emergency these stations would come into their own had the Germans successfully gained a foothold along the south coast of England and progressed as far as London. British forces would have fallen back to a prepared defence line in the Midlands where they would have regrouped and then been reinforced with forces from overseas before making a major counter attack.

16

TOP SECRET

Dates

~~May~~ 1940. State of Stations VIs and personnel.

HQ. personnel. about 30	VIs about 150	GPO Stations		
		HQ	5 single positions	
		Ballygomartin N.I.	4 positions	
		Thurso	1	D/F
		Lydd	3	D/F
		Sandridge	1	D/F
		Cupar	1	D/F
		St Erth	2	D/F
		Bridgwater	1	D/F

May 1940 — Barnet Intercept Station opened with 12 double positions (Ballygomartin NI closed down)

November 1940 — St Erth increased to 6 positions. all nine VI Regions functioning strength about 1600

January 1941 — Thurso increased to 4 positions

February 1941 — Unit training at Trowbridge for Egypt

March 1941 — Unit embarked for Egypt.

June 1941 — Hanslope opened with 32 double positions. VI's by this time over 1500 strong. HQ personnel now about 150 strong.

October 1941 — St Erth increased to 12 positions. Thurso increased to 12 positions

January 1942 — Gilnahirk opened 12 positions? Mobile units (3?) now at Barnet. Newcastle and Gilnahirk. Overseas units at Gibraltar 6 position. Cairo ? positions with some personnel at Teheran. ~~and Palestine~~.

End of 1942 — Units organised in India.

1943 — Forfar opened with 32 double positions. Barnet now 32 positions. Barnet Training school for operators organised. HQ Staff was about 250. Mobile units now at Bristol

[aircraft unit 12 positions formed in Rome]

1944 — mobile unit # organised with small intercept staff later goes to Normandy. Research station opened at Barnet.

TOP SECRET

26

he explained that he was a student during this period in time at the Municipal College of Technology Belfast and he recalled several electrical engineering lectures being cancelled when one of the lecturers, Thomas Palmer Allen, was called away to the Gilnahirk site to try to overcome some high voltage transmission problems. This problem of electrical supply was something that would revisit the Gilnahirk site again in 1944.

This aerial photograph from 1948 provides an excellent overview of the complete wartime site. The station consisted of five buildings, three brick-built and two wooden, plus the underground cabin. Having shown this photograph to a number of individuals who remember the wartime site all confirmed this is the site as they remembered it.

Like all the RSS stations during those early months of the war, when the Gilnahirk wireless station became operational its assigned task was to search the airwaves for any illicit wireless signals, a process conducted under the term 'general searches'. Each of the twelve banks, (working positions) within the wireless station would have been allocated a given frequency range over which the operator would have trawled back and forward time and time again. Each time he came upon a

Radio operator at work – although I regrettably have no images from inside the hut at Gilnahirk, I am assured that this image is broadly representative of it

signal the operator would record every detail possible from the frequency, the time the date and of course the Morse content of the transmission. It sounds like a soul destroying task, but it had to be done. Each transmission was recorded onto a paper log sheet and this was then sent by telex to the RSS headquarters which would work with other establishments such as Bletchley Park in a process of cataloguing, cross referencing, sifting and prioritising before attempts at de-coding would even begin so as to squeeze the greatest possible value of information out of the signals which had been intercepted.

While the core of the signal interception operations were the three radio listening stations at Thurso, St. Erith and Gilnahirk, they were only a part of the bigger picture which brings us to the next part of our story – the VIs.

O ne of the greatest problems facing the RSS at the time of its formation was how to quickly set up a network of listening posts which would stand any chance of picking up transmissions made by enemy agents.

During WW1 wireless technology was in its infancy and largely confined to the medium and long wave regions of the radio spectrum which were easily detected over a wide area centered on the transmitter which can thus be located relatively easily and quickly.

However by the late 1930s technology had moved on and shortwave transmitters were relatively common which made interception of any illicit signal much more difficult (see below). Right from its earliest day the RSS realised that it could not rely solely on a small number of listening stations such as Gilnahirk and that it would have to establish a geographically dispersed listening network to give it any chance of success.

Setting up a dispersed network of listening stations was one thing – getting the staff to man them was another. Within the ranks of the military highly qualified radio operators were at a premium as the war effort got fully into gear and thus to get the staff it required the RSS had to think outside the box and the concept of the Voluntary Interceptor (VI) was born.

Lord Sandhurst of the RSS realised that dispersed among the civilian population were many individuals such as radio amateurs, who would have the necessary skills and often also the equipment to set up listening posts in their own homes.

Amateur radio enthusiast Bob Barr who became a VI with his set in 1925

The difficulty in intercepting an illicit radio signal and using it to locate the transmitter increases significantly if the transmitter is broadcasting in the shortwave part of the radio spectrum rather than in the medium or long wave ranges. This is due to the way radio waves propagate between a transmitter and receiver located on the earth's surface. With WWII technology the two types of propagation which were available for long distance wireless communication were ionospheric propagation and ground wave propagation. To propagate via the ionosphere, the radio waves travels up to the ionosphere (an ionised layer at the outer edge of the atmosphere) from whence they are refracted back to the earth's surface some distance from the transmitter leaving a zone in between (known as the skip or silent zone) where no signal can be received. Radio waves in the short wave band are particularly well suited to propagation via this route and even a low powered transmission can be picked up at great distance. Ground waves, due to electrical interaction with the earth's surface tend to follow the curvature of the earth allowing them to be picked up well beyond the horizon. The ground wave for a radio transmission in the medium or long wave band will retain its strength for long distances and can thus be picked up by a ground based listener located anywhere in a large area

cont over...

To see if this group could be tapped into Lord Sandhurst from the RSS, a gentleman of some standing in the world of amateur radio, invited Arthur Watts the then president of the Radio Society of Great Britain (RSGB) to come and see him at the RSS HQ Wormwood Scrubs Prison, London. He had just one question for Arthur: "Would it be possible to engage the services of your radio amateurs in some government work?" The answer: "More than willing to serve King and Country."

Although on the first of September 1939 the Post Master General had issued a government directive that all amateur radio transmitters had to be disabled by the removal and handing over to the GPO those valves which allows a transmitter to send a radio signal, the radio amateur was still free to listen. Lord Sandhurst realised that within the ranks of the RSGB, a nationwide organisation, was potentially an existing listening network spread across the whole of the British Isles already equipped with radio receivers and a knowledge of Morse code. This asset which could greatly enhance Britain's listening capability with little or no expense to His Majesty's government.

Arthur Watts was given a very brief outline of what was required and told to go away and share this information with his regional officers of the RSGB.

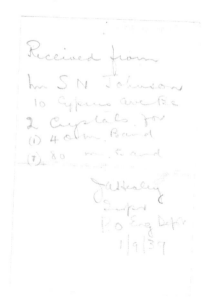

A more trusting age or the expediency of war? – A simple GPO receipt been kept by the family of GI5SJ Stanley Johnson from East Belfast. The receipt confirms that two crystals have been handed over to the Post Office engineering department for safe keeping. Assuming we win the war Stanley should get these items back

Recruitment

In each of the RSGB regions (including, I believe, Northern Ireland), the regional officer of the RSGB would then draw up a list of his fellow amateurs who he knew had a Morse receiving speed that would meet the requirements of the listening operation. The RSGB regional officer would then meet the RSS regional officer and a list of potential recruit names would be handed over for the vetting process to begin. Once that hurdle had been successfully crossed a letter of invitation would be sent to the respective radio amateur from the RSS regional officer.

The RSGB regional officer for N. Ireland at the time was Thomas Palmer Allen or TP as he was known to his friends. Based on various interviews with his daughter and associates from the Municipal College of Technology Belfast where TP lectured in their electrical engineering department, I believe TP worked closely with Capt. Joe Banham from the moment Banham arrived in Belfast. In time he became a VI himself although there is a rather strange anomaly which I am rather confused about. Across the British Isles radio amateurs and others who were recruited into the RSS as Voluntary Interceptors were allocated a regional number and on the back of a family photograph of TP is the number NI/24. In Northern Ireland all numbers began with NI/ followed by the actual number at the time of recruitment. Given his relationship with Captain Banham I would have assumed he was one of the first VIs recruited in N. Ireland yet his number seems to indicate that 23 had been recruited before him. Perhaps his official registration was recorded sometime after his actual recruitment or perhaps he only took up duties as a VI after he had completed the task of identifying other potential candidates. Whatever the reason, it would appear that by the end of 1939 there were a minimum of 24 VIs up and running in N. Ireland.

cont...

surrounding the transmitter. However at short wavelengths the electrical interaction with the earth's surface rapidly drains energy from the wave and the signal becomes undetectable only a short distance from the transmitter. If we consider a hypothetical spy working for the Germans monitoring naval activity in the Foyle and signalling the information back to his masters using a low power HF transmitter the problem becomes clear. As the transmission is in the shortwave region of the radio spectrum, the ground wave component of the signal will rapidly fade to nothing whilst the component being bounced of the ionosphere may be received clearly in Germany. For the listeners at Gilnahirk situated (as may be much of the UK) in the skip zone of the transmission, they will hear nothing as the ground wave will have faded out long before it reaches them and the ionospheric component of the signal passes far overhead and out of reach. The only chance of picking up the signal is to have someone listening in, tuned to the right frequency and located close enough to pick up the ground wave component of the signal before it fades away.

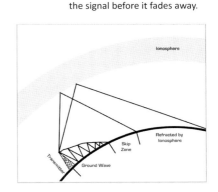

JULY, 31st. 1940.

REGIONAL OFFICER,
N.I. REGION,
RADIO SECURITY SECTION,
ROOM NO. 3.
TELEPHONE HOUSE,
CROMAC STREET,
BELFAST.

Dear Mr. Irwin,

              A large number of Amateurs have offered their services in a voluntary listening capacity.

              The Government has accepted this generous offer and has decided to extend the scheme so as to include all those who wish to give a few hours of their spare time as voluntary listeners.

              If you are interested I should be pleased to call at any time convenient to you and give further details.

              The whole thing is entirely voluntary and no pay is attached.

Yours sincerely,

J Banham

Capt.

When potentially suitable candidates for the program were identified they were then security vetted before any formal approach was made. Often this was by letter such as the one opposite received by Arthur Irwin of Ballygowan in Co. Down.

Arthur was a keen amateur radio enthusiast before the war but in accordance with the directive from the Post Master General he had ceased to broadcast on 31 August 1939 as evidenced by the entry in his log book at 22:50 'QRT for War' (QRT stands for 'stop sending')

Some eleven months after he is taken off the air Arthur received a short letter from Captain Joe Banham inviting him to become a Voluntary Interceptor. Captain Banham's letter confirms that a large number of amateurs have already offered their services in a listening capacity. One assumes Banham is referring to local recruitment and not national. Banham goes on to indicate that if you are interested, please get in touch. The onus is firmly on Arthur, there is no pressure, this is a purely voluntary service and furthermore it is made perfectly clear that you will receive no payment for your time and effort. The communication is short and to the point, but reveals nothing of the detail about what may be involved if Arthur accepts.

For others the approach was more clandestine. During my research I interviewed Bill Austin from Bangor, Co. Down and my notes of the interview follow.

"Bill Austin was taking in the sea air at Queens Parade Bangor when he was approached by a gentleman in military uniform. Bill was first asked if he had any knowledge of Morse code, to which he replied yes. The officer then asked if Bill would be interested in working for the government doing some vital war work. Bill's answer was again yes.

Amateur radio enthuasist Arthur Irwin signs off for the war.

Bill Austin

The officer then asked Bill to meet him again on the following Sunday morning at Bangor railway station, but to say absolutely nothing to anyone. At the appointed time both Bill and the officer boarded a train for Queens Quay terminus in Belfast. At Queens Quay they were joined by a second gentleman also in military uniform. All three boarded a tram for the Lagan Bank Road where they transferred to a bus with a destination board displaying, "Mann's Corner". The journey took around thirty minutes and on arrival at Mann's Corner, Bill and the two officers got off the bus and walked a short distance to what was clearly a military establishment. They were as Bill recalls well into the country at a place he had never heard of.

Having entered one of the brick buildings Bill was ushered into a room where he was invited to relax for a few minutes before taking up a position in front of a radio receiver placed on a table. Also on the table, a set of wireless headphones, pencils and some radio log sheets. Bill was about to undergo a Morse receiving test. Having placed the headphones over his ears he began to record the incoming Morse code. This process continued for some time. Throughout the process the speed of the incoming Morse code would increase but Bill could no longer keep up. It was all too much and sadly Bill did not have the skill to record on paper what he was hearing in his ears. Bill was escorted back to Bangor railway station where he was told by the departing army officer that he must forget everything that has happened today and speak to no one of it."

Bill Austin had just been tested to determine if he was suitable to become a Voluntary Interceptor. Bill could not recall the date nor the time of this event in his life but I know it had to be sometime after May 1940. Many years later, Bill married and settled in the Castlereagh area of East Belfast. Whilst out driving one day with his wife and children Bill unexpectedly came upon the wartime location again and suddenly realised where he was. How different his life might have been had he passed that Morse test?

The Work of the VI

Once a radio amateur signed the official secrets act he was no longer a radio amateur. He had become a Voluntary Interceptor and was now expected to spend a minimum of two hours in any given twenty-four-hour period in front of his radio set. Although the VIs were expected to do a minimum of two hours in any given twenty-four hour period we know that many did a great deal more. George Wright of Newtownards told me that on many occasions during the war his father Albert would walk into the dining room whilst he was getting ready for school. His mother's first question time and time again, "Have you been on that radio all night?"

However, when they volunteered the VIs were sworn to secrecy and could talk to no one outside the RSS about their work George's father said absolutely nothing and continued to eat his breakfast as if he were the only person in the dining room.

During his duty the VI would also have been given a frequency range which he was expected to trawl back and forward with everything he picked up recorded onto paper log sheets. This was no easy task for when the RSS listener placed his headset over his ears and began to search the airwaves he would have been confronted with a cacophony of sound. A mixture of voice, music, static and Morse were all mixed up together. Some sounds would have been loud and clear, some coming and going, others weak and distant. To lock into one faint distant Morse coded signal and blot out everything else required intense concentration.

Given that many of our VIs would have held down a normal job as well, that many served as VIs right throughout the war years is testament to their stamina and dedication.

From their induction into the work of the RSS the VIs had to use their own radio receivers, often simple Eddystone Shortwave Two sets, to conduct their general searches. Fine tuning and remaining on a given frequency was difficult at times if not impossible.

Eddystone Short Wave radio set

National Radio Company HRO Radio set. For different frequency bands this radio had different sets of tuning coils that slid into a full-width opening at the bottom of the front panel (alternative coils are sitting on the table front right). Before each radio left the factory its accompanying coils were calibrated for that particular radio. Together with a micrometer-type dial, these features allowed for great frequency resolution.

As Bob King (G3ASE) an English VI and full-time recruit of the RSS stated, *"you needed three hands on occasions to remain on station."*

It soon became clear that the VIs must be given the proper tool for the task in hand. During the early years of the war the standard wireless receiver used by British forces was the American HRO receiver. This was considered to be the Rolls Royce of its day and had a fine tuning capability that was second to none. As the stocks of this receiver began to grow within the British Isles the VIs were added to the list of those who needed this weapon of war urgently.

When I talked to Clive Bell, the son of Joshua Bell, a VI who lived in Mountcashel Street, off the Springfield Road in Belfast, he told me his father's HRO set was delivered by Captain Banham and it was like a Christmas Day. His father was over the moon. The set arrived in a large wooden create and included the power pack, head phones and a series of interchangeable tuning coils. Clive said that his father soon had arrangements in place to run a much longer aerial from the family home

The VIs were supplied with a residential telephone service assuming they did not already have one but this would have been used only in emergencies where a signal had been picked up that was considered urgent such as if the VI had heard the distress call of a pilot ditching in the sea.

Telephones were not the only perk. VIs were also entitled to an extra petrol ration. One assumes this was to cover their journey's to and from regular VI meetings hosted by Captain Banham when travelling on a bus or train would not have been considered appropriate. Clive Bell was able to tell me that these meetings took place on a regular monthly basis, especially in the Belfast area and his father made a point of attending them all. It was on these occasions that our VIs got to wear their Home Guard uniforms. If what Clive has told me is correct and I recall Pamela Allen stating something similar, the excuse to the family was simply given as Home Guard duties – no further information was given.

What follows is a copy of an invitation sent to TP Allen.

```
                                    N.I. REGIONAL OFFICE, R.S.S.,
                                       "HEATHCOTE", SANS SOUCI PARK,
                                          MALONE ROAD, BELFAST.
BELFAST 67275.

              We should like to see you at the next meeting of V.I's.
         which will be held in the Carlton Restaurant, Belfast, on SATURDAY,
         the 8th NOVEMBER, commencing at 8 p.m.

              Please let me know as soon as possible if you will be
         able to attend.

                                    (Sgd.) J.E.C. BANHAM, Captain.
                                                        R.Signals.

29th October, 1941.
```

I would assume the meetings allowed Banham to share his concerns on procedures, bring everyone up to date with the process, but more importantly it allowed our VIs to voice their concerns on various issues.

For the vast majority of the material they were listening out for, as stated above, the VI records it on paper log sheets. These log sheets were then placed into a plain brown envelope which was sealed and folded before being placed into a second plain brown envelope addressed to PO Box 25, Barnet. Assuming the VI lived in Belfast or a large town the envelope was then dropped into a standard street letterbox as soon as possible. I was informed by the daughter of one VI that her father was to use only the letterbox closest to their home.

During my research I came across the following two interesting snippets in the BT archives regarding telephone provision for VIs.

BT Archive: Section 4.2 Appendix 85. (Table one) is a half yearly summary of the number of cases dealt with in arranging with the Telecommunications Department the lists of RSS Voluntary Interceptors accorded preference subscriber facilities in order that they should be free during emergency periods, to make urgent reports by telephone in connection with their work as Voluntary Interceptors. (Table two) Priority to Voluntary Interceptors in respect of telephone service on the grounds that Voluntary Interceptors were important units in the RSS organisation I came across one example of an emergency.

BT Archive: Section 5.1 RSS Control General. RSS complain that a Voluntary Interceptor had difficulty in contacting the Post Office Inspector at RSS HQ to whom he desired to report an S.O.S. call.

above: Dr Joe Parke's cottage at Cloughy
below: The mysterious address

Arrangements had been made with the Post Office to have this letterbox emptied regularly as any delay in passing the completed interceptions of a VI on was not acceptable. For those in the country areas the Post Office had made an arrangement with the Ulster Transport Authority that people could post their letter by handing them to the bus conductor who would take them to the dispatch office where they would be picked up by a Post Office employee and taken to the central sorting office in Royal Avenue.

At the central sorting office all the mail addressed to the mysterious PO Box 25 Barnet was separated from the normal mail to be picked up by a dispatch rider and taken to Gilnahirk Wireless Station where it was opened and the information recorded on the log sheets telexed to the mainland.

Although the contents of the log sheets were all sent by telex for speed, the actual log sheets were still sent on to PO Box 25 for notes to be added for the VI when the log sheets had been thoroughly analysed. It may seem strange, but this was the main means of communication between RSS HQ and their VIs on the ground. Each log sheet would be examined and marked up accordingly. eg: A signal that had been copied, but was of no value or interest was marked, 'Not Wanted', other entries on the same sheet may have been marked 'Wanted'. Other notes could indicate such things as that a signal on a given frequency had 'Moved to a different frequency' or time with details perhaps included.

These log sheets where then returned to the respective VI who had sent them in the first place and he in turn would take note of all that he had been asked to do. As the process continued VIs got wise to what was heard within their frequency range and when something was heard which was of no interest it was immediately discarded and

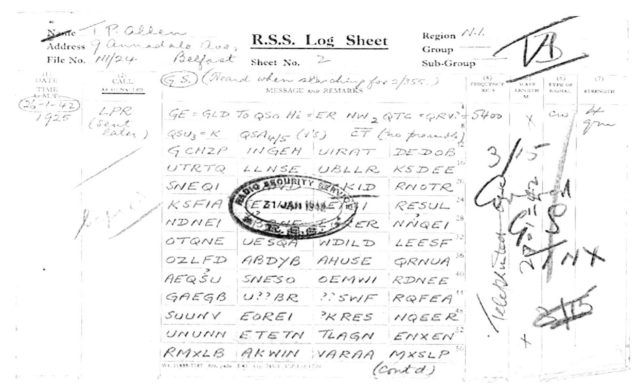

the search moved on. Unfortunately the process was not fixed and new transmissions were appearing all the time.

Sheets that were returned were then kept until Captain Banham came to visit. A strict record of all that had been sent and returned was kept. If ten logs had been returned they would be destroyed in the presence of Banham, security was tight and no indication of what they were doing could be allowed to leak out.

I have often wondered how much the VIs knew of the mysterious process that went on between them posting their log sheets to PO box 25 and getting back the marked up sheets. Or did they even know of the operation at Gilnahirk? Certainly some of the full-timers at Gilnahirk such as the teleprinter operator would have seen the names

Log sheet submitted by TP Allen and then returned marked up with comments.

and home addresses of our local VIs which were clearly marked on their radio log sheets but as to whether the VIs knew of Gilnahirk is more doubtful.

According to the families I've spoken to in the course of my research Captain Banham was a reasonably regular visitor – I wonder what cover stories were invented given the lengths many of the VIs seem to have gone to in hiding what they were doing given the heighten levels of suspicion in the general populace at the time although they were afforded some protection as the following information given to me by the family of a VI indicates: –

> "The VIs were registered with the Inspector General of the Royal Ulster Constabulary, not only as radio amateurs, but as conducting important war work. If the neighbour of a VI became suspicious of the listening activities, especially if the radio shack was placed in a back yard or down the garden with the light continually on in the wee small hours of the evening or early morning and this was reported to the RUC as the activities of a possible German spy. When the local constable appeared at the door of the VI's home and enquired of his behaviour he would present a card unto which was written a telephone number. The constable having phoned the number from the home of the VI would have got through to the RUC control in Belfast where a senior officer would inform the constable that all was well and instruct him to apologise to the VI for the visit and tell the complainant that she he had nothing to worry about."

Perhaps to wind up this section I should introduce you to some VIs. The following are a mix of my interview notes along with letters and other materials supplied by the VI's family.

Edgar's son kindly sent me this letter detailing his recollections of his father's wartime work for the RSS.

"My father Edgar Owen Byrne was appointed Manager of Ulster Bank, Clogher Branch in 1934. Prior to this during the 1914/18 conflict as a tank crew member he was badly wounded and gassed during the Battle of the Somme. Subsequently awarded the Military Medal he returned to civilian life and non-physically demanding banking because of war wound restrictions.

Clogher in those early days was very much an agriculture based community surrounded by large estates. People such as Colonel Gledstaines, Major Moutray, Colonel Garnett etc., were the local gentry and used my father's Branch to conduct their business affairs. Equally so did businesses such as Alan Johnson's hardware and agricultural equipment store which operated two large diesel generators, night and day, to give 230V DC power to the village. (It cost one shilling per unit!). Alan was a good friend of my father and when Dad decided to build a shed in 1935 to accommodate his developing ham radio activities Alan supplied the timber and fittings. This shed, always referred to as 'The Hut', was approximately seven feet square and located in a corner of a large gravel yard well away from the main house. 230V DC

above Edgar Byrne
below: Edgar's QSL card

was duly laid on as was a telephone to inform when tea was ready – although before long the phone mysteriously developed a fault and fell into disuse! A long wire aerial supported by a very tall pole at the hut end, terminating on a bank house chimney pot. It was in this setting before WW2 that dad constructed and operated his ham receiving and transmitting equipment – initially breadboard layout and later a tall wooden rack which housed six drawers. His success can be judged by the award to GI8LF of a 'Worked All Continents Certificate' using just 10 watts' power.

Sadly, all was to change in 1939 with the outbreak of WW2. The transmitting equipment was removed by the Government 'for the duration' – as a lad of just over four years of age I have faint memories of this. Later however I recollect happy times in 'The Hut' being shown how to solder, how to build a crystal set using a toilet roll centre as a coil former and also many hours of learning Morse code.

Edgar with his radio sets in 'the hut'

It is unclear now how much detail I remember directly from these early days and how much I learned from Dad and the family later. However, the arrival of an Eddystone 358 receiver is definitely well remembered and caused great excitement. It must have been Dad's first ever factory built equipment. Wearing headphones and sitting on the Hut floor under an old wooden table I listened to endless streams of Morse signals as Dad scribbled away up top. I know now that this must have been his RSS activity and I was only allowed to speak when he indicated. I tried so hard to read that Morse but only got the odd letter or number – fluency was achieved much later. It occurs to me now just how lonely Dad must have been night after night sitting with headphones on and the petrol stove hissing – maybe my pre-bed visits gave him comfort.

As the war progressed I remember a Captain Banham who became a regular visitor to our home and as a young lad saw him as just another friend of the family. His attempts to help my father gain more movement in his war wounded left arm and hand stand out particularly in my memory. These attempts were made by repeated squeezing of a soft rubber ball and also by trying to raise it further up the dining room wall. Another moment of excitement was the arrival of an HRO receiver and, towards the end of the war, Dad wondering if they would supply additional plug-in coils to cover all the ham bands. Instead, disappointment followed when a charge was made to keep the receiver.

The Hut

As the war progressed a further small receiver, an American Ecophone Commercial, appeared in our lounge and was positioned beneath a map of Europe. Each day my father would listen to the news and put pencil marks on the map to show advances / retreats of our troops. I still have the map.

Looking back now it is very noticeable just how much time Dad spent in 'The Hut'. At the time however it just seemed normal and everyone accepted that he was just mad keen on wireless. This belief was supported by his close friendship with Matt Mulcaghy (Wilson Guy – broadcaster and poet) who lived in Fintona. He was also a radio ham (GI3JP) and I understand that he spoke fluent German. It was also normal to see packages ready or in preparation for posting and seeing the pre-printed labels 'PO Box 25 Barnet' readily comes to mind.

At war's end the visit of Lord Sandhurst to our home made a double impression on me: the threat of severe discipline if we misbehaved, and seeing his facial (duelling?) scar. Years later Dad told me that Lord Sandhurst had thanked him for all the good work and also said that he had picked up signals from the German Pocket Battleship Scharnhorst which helped with its location and destruction.

So there it is, an outline of those, for me, cosseted and happy years of long ago. The players have moved on and now just memories remain – fragments from a fascinating period in our history.

Some WWII names of friends and visitors to our house
Trotter (no Christian name just 'Trotter') – Post Office Engineer and friend
Capt. Banham – frequent visitor
Lord Sandhurst – one visit
Matt Mulcaghy (Wilson Guy) GI3JP – friend
Sam Lister – friend
Dorothy Warnock ATS – friend
Lt. Danny Campbell RN – friend
District Inspector Joe Luke RUC and family – friends
PS: Dad was posted to Ulster Bank, Banbridge in 1947. Just before I left home there in 1952 I was rummaging in the loft and came across an old khaki uniform in a box. It was badly moth-eaten and turning to dust. I also discovered an old gas mask (the hose and canister sort). Can't remember if I mentioned it to Dad. This seems to tie in with what you said about the issue of uniforms to VIs.

As a cover for our Voluntary Interceptors in Northern Ireland they were all issued with Home Guard uniforms, but were not in the Home Guard. A number of the VIs, as well as doing their part time listening watches for the RSS, were also teaching Morse Code to many of the military cadet organisations. Some were also teaching Morse Code to the Home Guard. By wearing the uniform, it allowed them to blend in and be seen as doing their bit for King and Country.

It has never failed to amaze me just how much of the work of the Radio Security Service in Northern Ireland has been recovered. We read in this account so much confirming the memories and stories of other families whose fathers were also VIs. The recovery by the GPO of the transmitting coils or valves which disabled the radio set and made it a wireless receiver only; the visits by Captain Banham; the supply of an HRO American wireless receiver; most importantly the long hours spent by our Voluntary Interceptors seeking our German Abwehr enemy. The original two hours in twenty-four were not enough and the VIs were more than keen to go the extra mile or two.

At the end of the war Edgar must give his treasured HRO back, but you may keep it if you pay the asking price. Edgar's story confirms the recovery of those state of the art HRO receivers, something most of the VIs would have loved to retain. Surely considering the amount of unpaid time the VIs had given in service to their King and Country a blind eye could have been turned but no, the government wanted their pound of flesh in full. How mean can one be?

Thomas Palmer Allen (Voluntary Interceptor)

TP Allen at his radio (above) and his QSL card (below)

I first became aware of TP Allen through his daughter Pamela. The Somme Heritage Centre had arranged a week of lectures at which a number of guests would speak on subjects directly associated with Signals Intelligence. Vicky Warpole was the education officer at Bletchley Park, Ian Volkes came from the Royal Signals Museum and last but by no means least John Alexander an expert on encryption devices would also speak. Just prior to the week of the lectures, announcements had been made through the press and on the radio that the Somme was trying to recover information on the history and purpose of Gilnahirk Wireless station.

The majority of the lectures where held in the afternoons and on one particular day we had extended a warm invitation to the former staff members of post war Gilnahirk wireless station. To our amazement we had a packed house that day, but just before the lecture commenced I was informed by the one of the Somme staff members that there was a lady present who was very keen to speak with me. This lady was Pamela

Forsythe, daughter of TP Allen and after a brief introduction she and her husband Ian invited me to come and speak with them in person at their home in the Malone area of Belfast.

What that visit and other visits revealed was proof that the Radio Security Service had two separate listening operations going on in Northern Ireland at the same time. At Gilnahirk we had the full-time professional listeners but standing alongside this vital war work were a group of part time listeners. Until I met Pamela I had no real proof of their existence.

Her father had been involved with amateur radio as far back as 1926 when he and nine others had met at the Old Castle Restaurant in Belfast for the inaugural meeting of the Radio Transmitters Union of Northern Ireland and was well known among the radio fraternity of Ireland north and south. TP was also a lecturer in Electrical Engineering at the Municipal College Belfast, a position which through time granted him a Chair at Queens University Belfast. This interest in electrical engineering extended to Wireless Telegraphy where TP was personally involved with the classes that an individual had to attend if he desires a licence to operator a wireless transmitter or a higher qualification as a professional radio operator.

What transpired from my talks with Pamela revealed that TP had worked very closely with Captain Joe Banham from the day and hour he arrived in Belfast and together had been instrumental in establishing the Voluntary Interceptor network in the Northern Ireland. A nephew told me that TP had been prevented from joining up because of his electrical engineering background and should Belfast suffer a major loss of high voltage distribution through the blitz TP was one of a team appointed to restore the power to our Belfast industries as quickly as possible.

TP was, I am sure, one of the first to be selected as a Voluntary Interceptor but his relationship with Banham must have been excellent for Pamela produced for me a whole series of RSS Log Sheets that her father had managed to retain after the war. It was normal practise that such material be destroyed as quickly as possible after it was returned to the VI. These log sheets give us a first-hand account of what the VIs were doing from their own homes but more importantly will act as a record for the generations to come.

The majority of the log sheets TP had retained were completed at his uncle's home (The Boyd Family) at 9 Annadale Avenue in Belfast. After the first blitz on Belfast TP had taken the decision to move his wife and two daughters to a relation's summer cottage on the shores of Strangford Lough. Some of the log sheets are addressed accordingly as 'Cuan Cottage' Killinchy. In relation to the twenty odd log sheets which TP had retained I asked Pamela why he had done this. Her answer was simple; she did not know. In fact, it was only during the final days of his life that TP spoke to Pamela about his war work. She was informed of a large brown envelope, in which she would find some interesting material.

TP Allen's listening posts at 9 Annadale Ave (above) and Cuan Cottage (below) – unassuming outposts which reached into the heart of the Reich during the war against the Nazis

I sent copies of the material to Bletchley Park in the hope that it would make its way to the code breakers, but unfortunately the encryption on the wartime sheets remains a mystery.

Pamela was able to recall two wartime events which remain vivid in her mind. Both took place at Cuan Cottage, Killinchy. The first revolves around a listening watch her father was conducting late at night. TP got very excited as he listened to a particular Morse transmission. He revealed to his wife and the girls that the individual sending the message was someone he had previously been in contact with prior to the outbreak of war. The signal was coming from a Norwegian operator, but no name was given. It was the 'fist' of the individual that TP had recognised as familiar. Unfortunately, we know absolutely nothing more about this transmission except to say it was sent at the time of or shortly after the German invasion of Norway. The second event revolved around a particular visit by Banham when he had brought a captured German spy radio set to show her father. It was contained within a suitcase and she recalls being allowed to play with it.

Before I close this brief account I would like to add a few other aspects of TP's service to King and Country during the war. All over the nation certain individuals were appointed by the War Office as head hunters. Within the military, industry and other aspects of life there were from time to time a need for individuals with particular skills. The word would be passed out and these head hunters would go looking and start asking questions. I am told that TP was a head hunter for Queens University and provided the names of all sorts of individuals for various jobs and tasks during the war. Many of those who went from N. Ireland to Bletchley Park were identified by TP.

Albert Wright (Voluntary Interceptor)

Throughout my research I have enjoyed some unusual experiences, things that some would consider unbelievable. One such experience happened at the end of my first ever public lecture in my quest to uncover the names of our local Voluntary Interceptors. Bangor Probus club were holding their monthly meeting at the Somme Heritage Centre and it had been arranged that they would be the first to hear my lecture. As I spoke I mentioned various things that caused one of the members to recall memories from the war. George Wright was only a young lad during the war, but he remembered that his father was a keen radio amateur, in fact his father was a professional radio operator.

Albert Wright and the family home near Dundonald

When his father got married his new bride insisted that he give up his life at sea as a merchant navy radio officer and obtain a job on shore. This he did and was soon working for the Eire government's civil aviation authority. War was declared in September 1939 and it was not long after that Albert in his new job began to hear the distress calls of Britain's merchant ships that were being sunk by the German U-Boats. In a number of cases Albert knew the merchant navy radio officers who were sending the distress calls and as he began to learn of more and more deaths of those who were once his colleagues at sea he decided enough was enough.

He moved his wife and children north of the border and obtained a job with the Air Ministry at Nutts Corner. Albert was keen to do his bit for King and Country. Prior to the war Albert had been very open about his radio amateur hobby and had encouraged his children to come and listen to the incoming Morse which he would translate. Without warning that all stopped and the door to his radio shack was both closed and locked at all times. He made it clear to his wife and children that he was never to be disturbed if he was on his radio and that included the house burning down. This all happened shortly after the family moved into a large house on the outskirts of Dundonald, between Belfast and Comber.

On occasions when George was having breakfast his father would be confronted with questions from his mother like,

"Have you been on that radio all night? Do you never consider coming to bed?"

To which there was no reply. This happened on a number of occasions, but Mrs Wright never received an answer. That was not the only strange occurrence George experienced. His father had a Home Guard uniform of which the jacket and beret were hung in the hallway, but his father had no association with either the Home Guard in Dundonald or Comber, most strange to say the least. In fact, his father only wore the uniform when making the occasional evening visit to Belfast. The reasons for which were never revealed.

At the end of my first lecture the members of Bangor Probus congratulated me on an excellent talk, but George Wright stood up and declared to all present that I had just resolved a family mystery from the war years. Listening to all that I had revealed and remembering his late father's behaviour George was able to say with confidence that his father was a Voluntary Interceptor. I could not believe my good fortune, my first lecture and my first VI as a result. This was indeed a good omen for the future.

I arranged to meet George for a good question and answer session and it was soon confirmed that his father Albert Wright had indeed been associated with the work of the Radio Security Service as a Voluntary Interceptor, but there was a further mystery which has not been resolved to this day. Albert had taken young George to Gilnahirk wireless station on visits, and his father had talked about Gilnahirk wireless at various times. I unfortunately cannot prove it, but I believe Albert may have been recruited as a full-time radio operator when Gilnahirk became Station No 4 after October 1942. He may have told his wife and children he was still working for the Air Ministry at Nutts Corner, but from sometime in 1942 until the end of the war I firmly believe Albert was working as a full-time radio operator at Station No 4.

At the end of the war many of the Post Office operators who wore a Royal Signals uniform for the RSS returned to their civilian jobs with the Post Office. Albert Wright was again working for the Air Ministry after the war at Nutts Corner which further suggests he may have been on loan to Station No 4.

In the early 1950's the Air Ministry underwent a major review and as a result a great many of the Air Ministry radio stations were closed down. Albert resigned and began his own business rearing chickens, a business that would in time grow to become 'Wrights Chicks' of Newtownards.

Other Voluntary Interceptors

There are a number of VIs that I can record in name only, but for others it would be disrespectful of me not to mention some of the stories I have recovered in connection with their wartime service.

Dr. Joe Parke, of Cloughey, County Down. (GI8PA)

His family home 'Wayside' overlooked the Irish Sea. As we know it was essential that the VIs passed on their completed log sheets as quickly as possible and down the Newtownards Peninsula during the war the Ulster Transport Authority's bus service would act as agents for the Post Office. On all of the buses the conductor carried a Royal Mail leather pouch into which anyone could post a letter. You stood at the bus stop, signalled the bus to stop and without boarding the bus you could hand over your mail to the conductor and he would then place it into his leather pouch. It may have been Bangor or Newtownards, or even Belfast but when that bus reached the end of its journey that

Dr Joe Parke (above) and Dr William Kerr (below)

leather pouch was handed into the parcels office where it was then collected by someone from the Royal Mail and the contents were processed for delivery in the normal way.

The story goes that come rain, hail or shine Joe Parke stood faithfully waiting for the bus. There may have been a force ten gale blowing off the Irish sea on a bitterly cold and wet winters day, but Joe stood his ground. On numerous occasions neighbours and friends travelling on the bus would invite Joe to leave his brown envelope with them so that he may return home to the comfort of a warm fire. But Joe was a loyal and faithful servant fulfilling his duty correctly and as required. It was his responsibility to see those RSS Log Sheets on their way and despite the difficulties Joe never once shied away from his duty.

Joe Parke was one of the VIs whose work did not finish with the end of the war and, now working for the newly formed GCHQ he spent many evenings listening to the Russian traffic during the 1950s and 60s.

Dr. William Kerr, Kings Road, Knock (GI2KR)

Allister his son informed me that his father worked as one of a pair of VIs. Both VIs covered the same special watches, both covered the same frequency span. I could suggest the name of the other half of this working duo but I would be wrong to do so in case that was not the individual.

Allister went on to say;

"At the end of the war my father with a number of other VIs was invited up to the Wireless Station at Gilnahirk. There he had the chance

to examine a German Spy Radio set contained within a suitcase. To say he was impressed would be an understatement, the compactness and quality of the radio receiver was second to none." The reason for this gathering is unclear but it may have had a connection to Lord Sandhurst's visit to Northern Ireland when he came personally to thank the VIs for their contribution during the war.

William Kerr was also a post-war VI listening to the Russian traffic during the 1950s and 60s.

Dr Desmond Downing, Hawthornden Road, Knock (GI3ZX)

Recruited in 1940 Desmond did just one year as a VI before moving on to higher things with the Radio Security Service. According to Pat Hawker who served in a number of the Special Communications Units and a real authority on this subject reveals that Desmond went to England where he ended up working at the intercept station known simply as the Lodge on the road to Wolverton. This was part of the Hanslope station. Desmond shared a room with Pat and others. Within a few months Desmond was commissioned and posted overseas to work for the RSS in India. There he was a member of the SCU 11 and 12 based in Dhakuria in Calcutta. These two units were closed down in early 1946 and Desmond returned to England. He was eventually released from military service in September 1946 with the honorary rank of Captain.

Pat Hawker informed me that whilst at Queens University Belfast Desmond would make occasional trips across the border into Eire. MI5 had asked Desmond to do a little coat trailing whilst in Dublin with the purpose of baiting the local Abwehr agent. Unfortunately, nothing came of this.

Desmond Downing was a post war VI listening to the Russian traffic during the 1950s and 60s. His daughter Wendy recalls summer holidays to the north Antrim coast. First thing into the car every time, much to the annoyance of her mother, was her father's radio equipment, other things could be left behind, but not his radio. On arrival at their holiday cottage it was that radio which took precedence over everything else.

Dr Eric Megaw GI6MU

From his earliest years Eric Megaw had a fascination for radio and by the time he graduated from Queen's University in Belfast in 1928 his aptitude for the subject was recognised and awarded a research fellowship to research 'improvements in thermionic valves'. Joining GEC in 1930 where he began work developing the cavity magnetron, an essential component in early airborne radar.

Very much a team player, Megaw shied away from the lime light but as Sir Edward Appleton noted "those who were in the business knew well how much the practical development of the cavity magnetron for operational use was due to Dr Megaw. Yet, smilingly, he let the credit go wholly elsewhere".

However as his work on both the cavity magnetron and short wave radio propagation continued throughout the war his contribution did not go unnoticed and in 1941 he was summoned to Buckingham Palace to receive an MBE from the King. Given the vital strategic importance of this work I find it difficult that the War Office would permit him time to stand radio watch, eavesdropping German signals – yet at least two sources including the late Martin Armour, former senior manager with the Shorts Missile Division, have assured me that Dr Megaw was a VI!

Steve Dorman

Steve Dorman grew up in Portadown and had a lifelong interest in amateur radio. During his time at Campbell College he ran an amateur radio club and spent a fair amount of his spare time teaching Morse code to the military cadets and the Home Guard. When his studies in electrical engineering began at Queens University his technical abilities were soon recognised and he was quickly moved on to the University College London. The College moved away from London because of the Blitz to Leicester University. Despite the various moves his work as a VI continued, such was the importance of the listening process.

A letter to Leicester University from the RSS asking for absolute privacy for his work as a VI. In time Steve would move on to SCU 1, working at Waddon Hall where he became involved in several highly sensitive research projects including one which attempted to electronically interfere with the V2 rocket's guidance system.

At the end of the war Steve moved unto the Diplomatic Wireless Service. He retired in 1981 a superintendent with Her Majesty's Government Communications Centre at Hanslope. This is not to be confused with GCHQ. Steve passed away in 1998 an unsung hero of WWII.

Jack Smyth 3 Alexandra Gardens, Portadown (GI3AOB)

Jack Smyth like those mentioned before had a life long association with amateur radio. As a technical school teacher he encouraged many of the pupils in his classes to take an interest in amateur radio and Morse Code. His daughters recall the house being visited by young men keen to gain additional knowledge and skills on all things wireless telegraphy and Jack was only too willing to oblige. He worked tirelessly within the cadet organisations training potential recruits for military service telling them all when enlistment came to mention your ability to understand Morse code. That will keep you out to the trenches he would say, but a great number of those he trained went on to become RAF radio operators with bomber command.

His service as a VI began in 1943 and lasted through into the post-war period listening to the Russian traffic during the 1950s and 60s.

J. Pinkerton, The High Street, Ballymoney. (GI8DB)

The Pinkerton family have had a long and distinguished association with the legal profession in Ballymoney with Jack serving a term as President of the Law Society in N. Ireland. As far as his daughter Pat was concerned Jack was an officer in the Home Guard and that was the sum total of his war service. When I first mentioned possible links to military intelligence and Bletchley Park, she was somewhat shocked, but her brother John had some wartime paperwork which he did not fully understand, but had his suspicions. When shown the paper work I was able to confirm that their father had indeed been a VI during the war.

Joshua Bell,

When I interviewed Clive Bell, son of Joshua Bell, he remembered that his father had created a radio shack in the roof space of their home at Mountcashel Street, off the Springfield road in Belfast prior to the war. Clive also recalls the erection of a very large V shaped aerial which ran from the chimney breast in two directions to the chimney breast of two houses at the rear of the house. But Joshua was not a radio amateur because everything was cleared out within a year of the war ending. His father was an assistant manager in the bread server department with the Co-Op bakery. He also mentioned a man called Banham who came to their home from time to time and always stayed for tea. He finally mentioned the delivery of an HRO receiver which his father compared to winning the pools. It was information like this which confirmed his father had links to the work of the Radio Security Service. Like the pieces of jigsaw puzzle I was able to explain the bigger picture to his son and reveal the truth of what his father had really been doing during the war.

Three other memories Clive shared with me. "Access to the roof space was strictly off limits expect when the ammunition (sharpened pencils) were running low. My father had created a pre drilled block of wood into which he had placed a series of sharpened pencils in the vertical position. This allowed him to select a new pencil quickly whilst listening to the incoming Morse coded message if the current pencil in use was no longer fit for purpose. As the stock of sharpened pencils went down the need to replace them was urgent and my father would bang a walking stick on the ceiling which was his sign for me to get up into the roof space quickly and start sharpening. Once the wooden block was full again I was instructed to leave the roof space."

A radio amateur's Fist. "My father could emulate the Fist or style of another radio operator, something he acquired a name for amongst other radio amateurs. His ability to listen and then repeat almost at once the way another radio operator tapped his Morse key was something most unusual, but a great asset if someone was trying to hid his Morse transmissions behind various call signs and frequencies.

A mystery, "To this day I still do not understand my father's departure from the family home. Out of the blue Banham arrived in his car and took my father away. My father took a suitcase with him did not return for about six or seven weeks and when he did return he was visibly drained, had lost weight and looked like someone who had been working around the clock. This period in time was never discussed, but sometime later I was rummaging about upstairs when I noticed for the first time a Royal Signals officers uniform in a wardrobe complete with shirt, socks, shoes, hat, everything but my father never served with the military full-time. My father also had a Home Guard uniform, but once again it was not something he wore on a regular basis. Some years after the war my father was watching an air show on television when a Lysander aircraft appeared on screen to which he made reference to its height off the ground, especially when getting out on a dark night."

Voluntary Interceptors Names.

We now come to those I can only mention by name, but that does not devalue the service they made to the work of the Radio Security Service during WWII. During my search to undercover the names of those who had served as VIs in Northern Ireland I knew there would be many I could never find. Sixty years had passed when my interest was kindled, but it would be a further two years before I learnt anything about Voluntary Interceptors. When I discover the names of VIs who were unfortunately no longer with us, and I soon realised I was going to find this process well nigh impossible. When these VIs signed the official secrets act they kept their VI duties from everyone and that included their families. When the war ended many expected to be released from their vow of silence, but the coming of the Cold War sealed their fate. British Military Intelligence who had engaged their services during the war were back with the Official Secrets Act again. The listening process was to continue and for many there would be no release. The majority would take all their secrets to the grave.

The names that I am about to reveal come from the entries in a book that contain the minutes of the Radio Transmitters Union of Northern Ireland. In the final pages of this book are a list of names. Against some of the names has been placed a red tick and when I first examined this book I noticed that of those VIs that I had confirmed myself, their names had a red tick. Could this be a list of our wartime VIs? I had spoken to Barney Patterson on this very topic when returning the RTU minute book to him. I had been allowed to digitally copy the pages but Barney said nothing. I then asked who was the last person to have this book before it was placed into his safe keeping and he answered Stanley Johnston. Some considerable time later when Barney's health began to deteriorate I got a phone call from him confirming my suspicions. Stanley Johnston a VI himself had gone through the list of those Radio Transmitters Union members and against those who had been Voluntary Interceptors during WWII he marked with a read tick. This list is not complete for some of those I have confirmed as being VIs are not on the list but it goes a long way to assist our understanding. For some with family connections this list will come as a shock, but it was a pity that those personally involved could not share with their own flesh and blood the contribution they had made to the work of Bletchley Park, but more importantly to the winning of WWII.

R. Carlisle, 1 Portstewart Road, Portrush (GI6WG).

F.E. Neil, Chesterfield, Whitehead, (GI5NY).

J.A. Sand, 22 Stranmillis Gardens, Belfast, (GI6TB).

W.H. Martin, 45 Bawnmore Road, Belfast, (GI5HV).

C.B. Cleland, 17 Forth Avenue, Bangor, (GI2CN).

T.S. Craig jnr, 43 Southwell Road, Bangor, (GI6TC).

B. McCann, 104a Divis Street, Belfast, (GI2KN).

R.J. Harvey, 144 Indiana Avenue, Belfast, (GI5DU).

F. McDowell, Osbourne Park, Belfast, (GI5MZ).

W. Graham, 8 Donegall Pass, Belfast, (GI5GV).

T. Maitland, 29 Marlborough Park Central, Belfast, (GI5SQ).

S. Johnston, 191 Holywood Road, Belfast, (GI5SJ) The author of this list.

R. Barr, 4 Dunkeld Gardens, Belfast, (GI5UR).

R.A. Sproule, Garvaghy, County Londonderry, (GI2SP).

J. Adams, 24 Northfield, Donaghadee, (GI5AJ).

J.N. Smith, 73 Oakland Avenue, Belfast, (GI5QX).

D. Meharey, Meadow bank, Whitehouse, (GI2OY).

W. Sullivan, Groomsport Road, Bangor, (GI6XS).

J. Cowden, Carnmoney, Belfast, (GI2BZV).

J.E. Maxwell, Kings Crescent, Belfast, (BRS1612).

W.J. Nicholl, Upper Newtownards Road, Belfast.

?. Wilson, Belmont Church Road, Belfast.

D. Waite, 10 ? Street, Belfast.

J.R. Savage, Ministry of Education, Belfast.

J.C. Thompson, Lisburn Road, ? (2ATC)

H. Waite jnr, 17 Willsden Park, Stranmillis,

L.L. Shene, Hopefield Avenue, Portrush. (2BRV).

J. Crooks, Queens Street, Belfast.

One final name I must add is that of **J. Martin GI3SG** who I am assured by his grandson was a Voluntary Interceptor during the war.

Others

Frank Robb (GI6TK) was another East Belfast VI. I know very little about this gentleman except to say he lived at Victoria Avenue, Sydenham

James (Jimmy) Cowan (GI5OY) was a VI from 1940 and lived at Weathfield Crescent, Ballysillan, Belfast

Fairly quickly after its inception it began to become clear that the whole raison d'etre for the RSS might be flawed. Set up as a primarily inward looking operation searching for radio transmissions from German Spies infiltrated into the UK it gradually became clear that the spy threat had been greatly exaggerated. Public perception was that the country was full of well-trained German spies whereas even for the last months of 1940 after the Abwher tried to ramp up its operations, the number of agents dispatched from Europe was in the low 20s and most were poorly trained and easy to spot.

Early successes for MI5's Double Cross System where by captured German Agents were quickly 'turned' to work for the Allies and feed false information back to Germany resulted in new agents often being instructed to make contact with agents who unknown to their previous masters were now working for the British.

During the past quarter, 11 "P" cases have been reported via the Post Office to R.S.S. and to M.I.5. ("P" cases see entry of 6th September 1939).

The total number of these cases for the past year is 44.

An early indication that the threat was not as predicted can be seen from part of an RSS minute which confirms only forty-four cases of Illicit Wireless transmissions during 1939.

Captured arriving agents also yielded a wealth of information on the hand ciphers used by the Abwher which enabled further penetration of the German intelligence operations.

When John Masterman, the head of the 20 committee which oversaw the Double Cross operation claimed in his 1972 book *The Double-Cross System in the War of 1939–45* that MI5 ran and controlled the German espionage system in the UK it was an accurate statement rather than an idle boast.

Based on a story relayed to me from members of the post war staff at Gilnahirk, Worlledge's misgivings about the semi civilian nature of the RSS operation in 1941were well founded. Apparently when Captain Banham arrived to work one day he was greeted by one Joseph Lenihan who was sitting having a cup of tea. Lenihan had been parachuted by the Germans into Eire with a view to making his way to England where he would report back on the war effort. However he decided to hand himself in in N.Ireland as he was wanted by the Garda. With the civil authorities in NI not knowing what to do with him someone seemed apparently had the bright idea of dumping him at Banhams office – possibly not the most security conscious move!
I initially took this tall tale with a pinch of salt but sometime later I realized that truth can be stranger than fiction when I uncovered these documents in the Kew archive!

A message has come through from Banham the R.S.S. man in Ulster that a man called Joseph LENIHAM, an alleged parachutist, was sitting in his office drinking a cup of tea. The story is that LENIHAM came down in Eire on Sunday, made his way across the border and gave himself up to the military. He has left his two-way wireless set in Eire but has with him an auxiliary one-way set. We have arranged that Cecil and T.A.R. shall go over in the morning and fetch him back to this country.

logue Reference:KV/4/188

Moore of the R.U.C. has come to an agreement with his contact in the Garda by which we are

Catalogue Reference:KV/4/188

.995

lent
to be lent LENIHAN's wireless set for 8 days. We are to lend the auxiliary one-way set to the Eire Govt for a similar period. Before the agreement was signed the matter was referred to Dev.

Cont opposite ...

Although the RSS had no success in tracking down illicit radio transmissions by spies in the UK, there being no spies to make them, they did achieve success in other unexpected directions.

When listening in on the frequencies expected to be used by German agents the VIs and full time listeners of the RSS had heard and recorded some mysterious weak Morse signals with unusual call signs and transmitted in groups of five letter code.

When these signals were analysed they were identified as emanating from various Abwher control centers in Mainland Europe the monitoring of which had the potential of providing invaluable insights into the thinking at the core of the German war machine.

As well as this change of focus from inward looking spy catchers to outward looking intelligence gathers by late 1940 some organizational problems were beginning to impact on RSS operations. Essentially these problems stemmed from the time of the RSS's inception when the urgency of getting something up and running quickly had necessitated farming out the work to the GPO. Although the GPO was technically highly competent, as an organization it brought with it a lot of baggage such peacetime work practices which, upheld by a strong union, were totally unsuited to critical wartime operations.

As such, despite all that had been achieved since the commencement of his remit, Colonel Worlledge, the officer in charge of the Radio Security Service, was not a happy man and on 11 February 1941 he wrote a rather plain speaking letter to his superiors in the War Office. (see appendix 2)

Colonel Worlledge firmly states that in his opinion the RSS as it stood was not fit for purpose due to a lack of clear chain of command and working practices resulting in a 'state of incompetence and inefficiency which would not be tolerated for one moment in any fighting service'.

His letter went on to suggest that unless the transfer of the RSS lock, stock and barrel was made on a proper military basis the future was not great. Worlledge wanted a purely military arrangement organised as one unit under King's regulations. It had to be one definite unit although he was prepared to compromise and allow the possibility of a mixed military and civilian unit if that was the only way forward.

Worlledge recognised that the acute shortage of wireless operators across the nation had not helped and any reorganisation of the RSS should ensure the retention of all the efficient operators and senior staff who were working in the RSS but currently employed by the Post Office. Those transferring into the new organisation would be assessed on their own merits and past record of efficiency. Worlledge wanted only the best as this was a highly specialised task and he had no intention of losing the experience and training that had been gained during the past eighteen months of war and to make sure this happened he suggests *'The authority of this process of transfer and seconding would rest solely with myself, the commanding officer.'*

Based on his own records and knowledge of the Post Office staff Worlledge expected to accept two thirds of the current work force which amounted to about two hundred operators which was some way short of the 450 staff he felt he needed. To fill these additional positions, he suggested drawing on *'those civilians, ex-amateurs principally, who are now and have been for many months employed as Voluntary Interceptors by the RSS'* who at the time numbered approximately 1,100.

In acknowledgement of the new focus of the RSS as an intelligence gathering operation Sir David Petrie, the Director General of MI5

July 25th

We had a conference about LENIHAN. We came to the conclusion that the only use we could make of his set would be by impersonation. LENIHAN was dropped in the Curragh with instructions to send weather reports to Sligo, and to proceed to England in order to obtain information about air raid damage. He had given himself up in N. Ireland because he had a criminal record in the south. He is wanted for unlawful assembly, presumably in connection with an I.R.A. meeting, and has also done time for fraud. The Irish have already discovered his parachute, and his set, which has not so far been taken, is left at a house on the Eire side of the border.

We had another meeting about LENIHAN and decided that we should abandon the idea of using his set. We propose to send a message in secret ink indicating that he has managed to get over here and has established contact with an I.R.A. friend in Liverpool. He will ask for instructions. We shall have to keep him permanetly at Ham but we may be able to work him through a cut-out.

Reports indicate that there is a shortage of essential products in Ireland.

July 30th

July 4th LENIHAN has been caught trying to get out of the country by joining the crew of a fishing-boat leaving Fleetwood, Hants. to fish off the coast of Donegal.

PRESENT STAFF   September 1942.

Station	Estab.	Name	ASE	EE	AE	CI	I	CO	SMT	SW1	SW2	Lab.	Total	R.
Headquarters	ASE	Hollinghurst, F.	1										1	
	EE	Wilson, F.		1									1	
	AE	Billington R.M.			1								1	
	I	Stiles, O.A.					1						1)	On loa
	I	Swann, G.F.					1						1)	M.I.
	CO	Court, R.						1					1	
	SWT	Lewis, R.A.(Miss)							1				1	
	SW2)													
	USW)	Bee J.R.								1			1	
TOTAL			1	1	1		2	1	1	1			8	
Kilnahirk Intercept.	CI	Streeter, A.R.				1							1	
	SW1										16		16	
	SW2)													
	USW)										15	2	15	
	Lab)													
TOTAL						1					29	2	32	
Kilnahirk Mobile	I	(Healey J.A.								1			1	
		(Mackenzie, T.G.								1			1	
	SW1										3	20		23	
	SW2)													
	USW)											3		3	
TOTAL										5	23		28	
Kilnahirk D/F	SW1									1	3		4	
										1	3		4	
Garnet Freq.Measuring	SW1										5		5	1 on loan to W2/3
TOTAL											5		5	
Wper D/F	SW1									2	3		5	
	Lab.											1	1	
TOTAL										2	3	1	6	
Thurso D/F	I	Honeyman, J.B.					1						1	
	SW1										5		5	
	USW										1		1	USW on loan to W2/3
	Lab.											1	1	
TOTAL							1				6	1	8	
Bandridge No.2 D/F	SW1									4	1		5	
TOTAL										4	1		5	
Bridgwater D/F	SW1									5	2		7	2 on loan to W2/3
	Lab.											1	1	
TOTAL										5	2	1	8	
..Erth D/F	SW1									1	4		5	
TOTAL										1	4		5	
......ham D/F	SW1									2	4		6	
TOTAL										2	4		6	
...verthorpe D/F	SW1									1	3		4	
TOTAL										1	3		4	
...lington Mobile Unit	SW2)													2 on loan to W2/3
	USW)										2		2	
TOTAL											2		2	

Grand Total   121

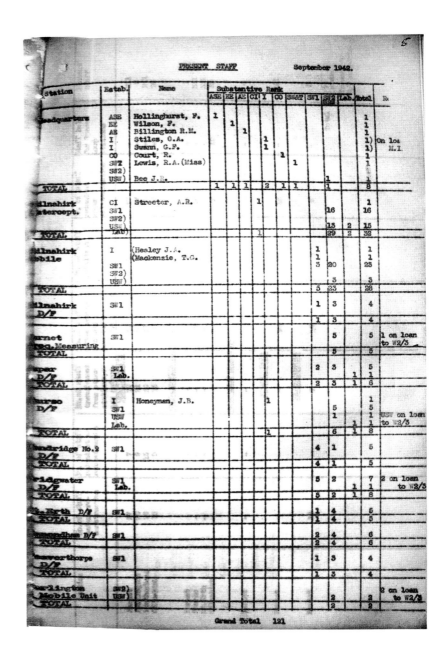

List of GPO staff working under contract for the RSS in late 1942

had recommended that *'That the RSS be equipped, staffed and run purely as an Intelligence instrument of MI6.'* A recommendation Colonel Worlledge accepted, provided proper plans were made and the necessary resources made available.

Clearly much of Colonel Worlledge's letter was accepted by higher command for in the closing months of 1941 the role of the RSS began expanding to take over all the work they had previously contracted out to the GPO.

During the early years of my research I had been advised that finding any evidence relating specifically to Gilnahirk would be almost impossible as vast amounts of documentation associated with the work of the RSS had been destroyed after the war for reasons of security and initially this important part of Gilnahirk's history looked destined to remain opaque.

You can thus imagine how surprised and delighted I was to learn that someone had overlooked a prime source of wartime information. At the time Colonel Worlledge was putting pen to paper the GPO was still under contract and providing almost everything the RSS required to complete their obligation to the War Office and as such, it was only natural that the GPO and the RSS would have on going meetings to resolve any issues which might arise as the GPO was phased out of the operation. The GPO naturally had minutes of these meetings (called Senior Officers Conferences) and retained copies in their archives. Everything here after marked 'Senior Officers Conference' comes for the BT Archive in London and gives a valuable insight of what was happening at the time.

From the minutes of these meetings it is clear that the future of Gilnahirk was coming into question.

There were several reasons why this may have been on the agenda but foremost was almost certainly Northern Ireland's unique position within the United Kingdom during WWII

1. On the mainland of Great Britain St. Erth in Cornwall and Thurso in Scotland can at the stroke of a pen become military establishments. All the GPO civilian staff will receive their call up papers and any employee of the GPO engaged in the work of the RSS will swear an oath of allegiance to the King, sign the Official Secrets Act, and don a Royal Signals uniform. For these new military recruits, they will step out of their civilian clothes at the end of one watch and then appear for the next watch in military uniform – although there will be no square bashing as these men are not in the army but are civilians employed by MI6. The wearing of a Royal Signals uniform would provide a cover to allow each and every one to blend in and be seen as doing their bit for King and Country. However in N. Ireland it would not be that easy. For political reasons it was the only part of the United Kingdom that did not apply the policy of conscription and asking GPO employees who lived

in nationalist areas to be seen to join the British military forces could cause massive problem for them and their families, no matter their own personal views.

2. N. Ireland was the only part of the United Kingdom with a land border to a neutral country, Eire. In the capital Dublin, Germany had established a legation and this along with the aspirations of the Irish Republican Movement was seen as a very serious threat to our national security. With relationships between Churchill and De Valera at an all-time low during the early years of WWII over the refusal by the Irish government to allow the Royal Navy use of the Treaty Ports, memories of the Easter Rebellion of 1916 during WWI had made many in the British establishment wary.

With these difficulties it may well have been considered simpler all round just to close the station down.

Item four on the agenda for meeting No 7 Senior Officers Conference dated Tuesday November 11th, 1941 read as follows.

Lieut, - Col. Lacey referred to the question of the closing down of the Gilnahirk Station and the taking over of St. Erth and Thurso as military stations under Special Communications Unit number three. He reported that during his visit to Gilnahirk, Mr Streeter, the chief inspector had produced a scheme under which he said that he would be able to obtain operators from Northern Ireland who were at present not subject to conscription. Many were ex ships operators, and he thought they would be willing to enlist for duty at Gilnahirk if it was continued as a military station. Leiut, - Col. Lacey said that he had passed on Mr Streeter's suggestions and proposals to the controller, who thought they were well worth examination and he would give them his careful consideration. The controller stated however that if Gilnahirk station continued if would be of a temporary nature, based on existing Post Office buildings and huts. It must entail only slight expenditure and would only be something extra to the three main permanent Intercept stations planned for Great Britain. Lieut, - Col. Lacey stated that the controller had instructed him to go further into the matter with Lord Sandhurst. Major Morton-Evans said that he hoped an additional station in Northern Ireland would be established as every available set that could be brought into use on a permanent basis would be an enormous help.
End of minute.

These opening remarks did not bode well for the continuation of Gilnahirk wireless station. Colonel Worlledge was clearly going to get his completely military organisation and the Post Office were to be phased out of the operation.

Seven days later the question of Gilanhirk is up for discussion again.

Senior Officer's Conference
Meeting No 8 – Tuesday November 18th 1941
Item D. GILNAHIRK
The controller reported that the whole question of employing Irish operators suggested by Mr Streeter depended entirely on security and that the matter was being considered from this point of view. He hoped to hear in the

near future whether the proposal was one which could be accepted on security grounds and would inform the conference as soon as possible.
End of minute.

These comments refer to the fact that the 'new' RSS was to come under the auspices of MI6, an organisation were absolute security was essential. The "Ultra" process was already in place and any breach, no matter how small could destroy everything that had been achieved. In short Northern Ireland was considered a liability.

Senior Officers Conference
Meeting No 9 Tuesday November 25th 1941
Item F.
Gilnahirk. The controller reported that he had no further news at the present with reference to the question of employing Irish operators as suggested by Mr Streeter. The matter was still being considered on the grounds of security.

Senior Officers Conference
Meeting No 10 Wednesday December 10th 1941
Item C. Gilnahirk.
The controller stated that he was afraid the answer would be "NO" on security grounds to Mr Streeter's suggestion of enlisting Northern Ireland personnel for the Radio Security Service. He explained that the station would be kept going as at present for the time being until it was closed down. Lieut. – Col. Lacey reported that Thurso and St. Erth were being changed over to military establishments and that Post Office personnel were being specially enlisted for this purpose. Mr Reardon would be commissioned and granted the rank of Captain an in charge of St. Erth. Mr McHarg would be moved from Gilnahirk to Thurso and would be commissioned with the rank of Lieutenant in charge. Mr Bennett would be moved from Thurso to the engineering section, Hanslope, with the rank of subaltern.

End of minute.

The writing was on the wall and the future of Gilnahirk looked bleak to say the least.

Unfortunately, at this point my research hit a wall or perhaps more accurately came to the edge of a chasm insofar as there is a gap in minutes of these meetings.

As with all aspects of my research, given the order by the director of military intelligence at the end of the War that all documentary evidence of what had taken place at Bletchley Park and the out stations must be destroyed at once leaving no evidence or trace of any kind on site, the surprising thing is that I have been able to find any minutes rather than that some are missing!

An indication of how valuable the trained radio operators were is given by the War Office's actions following the Belfast Blitz when a decision was made to bring all of the PO civilian staff (especially the radio operators) working at Gilnahirk out of the city and closer to the station site. This was achieved by an appeal being make from the pulpits of a number of local churches (Gilnahirk, Castlereagh, Dundonald, Knock and Comber). If you had a spare bed or a spare room and you were prepared to accommodate one or more you were to speak with your minister or your priest and he in turn will pass on your details to the RSS regional office. This appeal was well received and a number of local farms in the area were more than willing to accommodate the displaced staff. One local resident and neighbour of the station who accepted this call was Mrs Eleanor Martin of "Clondara House" a family farm only a stone's throw from the wireless station. A large wooden out building on the farm was very quickly cleaned, painted and made ready to accommodate an unknown number of Post Office staff. A system of rotation was put into operation and as one watch prepared to go on duty, beds were stripped, sheets and pillow cases were changed and everything was made ready for those coming off duty. As well as providing sleeping accommodation Mrs Martin also provided hot meals as required and packed lunches for those going on watch. I am told by those who recall this time that Mrs Martin's washing lines were continually full of sheets and pillow cases. She was a lady who was not afraid of hard work and knew the financial rewards of such labour.

To have found such documents would maybe have answered a great conundrum for me – why, after closure looking so certain at the end of 1941, on the other side of the chasm in the records Gilnahirk reappears operating full steam ahead in 1942?

Possibly the security concerns were overcome by recruiting more ex-military personnel. Maybe it was decided that the loss of trained and experienced personnel resulting from Gilnahirk's closure outweighed the security risk. Possible there was high level intervention from the N. Ireland Government …. the list is endless but is all speculation.

Whatever the reason by October 1942 the Gilnahirk Wireless station emerges as an integral part of the RSS under the control of and staffed by personnel who are now employees of Military Intelligence (MI8c) with plans afoot to expand the operation.

Undated entries from SCU minutes:

> **The Officer in charge of Gilnahirk Interception Station put forward detailed proposals for expanding Gilnahirk Interception Station on the existing site as an alternative to closing down the station in favour of a new and larger station. Col. Maltby comments that their proposals to replace Gilnahirk will be pursued.'**
> **At the RSS senior officers conference the controller stated that proposals from the Post Office O/S at Gilnahirk Interception Station to keep that station going with locally recruited operators depended entirely upon security and the matter was being considered from that point of view.**

Captain Banham is now proposing to use the brick buildings on site to create a bigger station as an alternative to building a new station, but security is still an issue.

Senior Officer's Conference Meeting No 21 – Wednesday July 29th 1942 Item 4

> **MOBILE UNITS**
> **Major Elmes reported that he proposed to commence enlisting the Post Office personnel at the Leatherhead and Darlington, Mobile Unit Bases on August 12th. As regards Gilnahirk, it was decided that the date of taking over these personnel should be deferred till the next meeting as**

it was considered advisable that the Mobile Unit personnel should be taken over at the same time as the Intercept Station at Gilnahirk was taken over by SCU 3. Major Sabine reported that he did not think he could have any operators ready for Gilnahirk before October 1st and Mr Hollinghurst said that he would have to consult Mr Mumford on this point as he had hoped that the Mobile Unit base would be taken over with the others. It was suggested that the twelve spare operators who were being retained for Spaced Loop Direction Finding could be enlisted if willing. Major Elmes reported that Captain Banham considered that he could obtain further volunteers from Northern Ireland for Gilnahirk station. The controller stated that the names of any volunteers from Northern Ireland must be submitted to him for special approval before being enlisted. Mr Hollinghurst reported that the first three Pantechnicon mobile units were ready and were being despatched to Gilnahirk. The remaining three which had been ordered would be issued to Barnet, Leatherhead and Darlington.

Seven months on and there appears to be a positive future for Gilnahirk Wireless station. Talk of closure is no longer on the agenda and Captain Banham is looking for further volunteers. The GPO is standing down and new arrangements for a completely new set of staff are on-going. It is clear that both the Mobile Units in Northern Ireland will be taken over at the same time as the Intercept Station. Promising news about the RSS operation in Northern Ireland comes with the expected arrival of three pantechnicon vehicles designed especially for the Mobile Units. I was told that these MU's spent a fair amount of their time along the border with Eire. One gentleman involved with these MU's was Billy Boston who lived on the Holywood Road, Belfast.

Senior Officer's Conference Meeting No 24 – Wednesday September 9th 1942

Item 14
GILNAHIRK
Major Sabine reported that he had arranged to send one Subaltern, two Sergeants and Twenty operators to Gilnahirk to take over the present Post Office station. All the operators were volunteers. It was proposed

Air Raid Warning Red

Despite their value to the war effort, when the air raid sirens sounded a warning for the pubic to take cover, our VIs were expected to man their radio receivers listening and searching for any signs of a radio beacon which may be directing the Luftwaffe onto their target. Such work for those who lived close to the docks, shipyards or areas of manufacturing within a large city was extremely dangerous and I was told a story of a VI who lived in the York Street area of Belfast who was killed whilst conducting his listening watch during one of the air raids on Belfast. Unfortunately, his name remains hidden to this very day.

to man six watch receivers, but he would not be able to man the three general search, which were at present manned by Mobile Unit personnel. Major Elmes stated that he hoped to take over four and possible eight of the existing Post Office for Mobile Units. The controller stated that it would be necessary to send over another complete crew from one of the English bases. Mr Wilson was asked to try and obtain additional Post Office personnel from Northern Ireland, especially those for the Spaced Loop Direction Finding. Major Sabine reported Captain Banham thought he could get additional names of men who would volunteer and would arrange that these names would be sent off as soon as possible for special vetting.

There is urgency in this minute that suggests all must be in place for a given date. Sadly, the date is not revealed. It is also clear from this minute that a number of local Post Office personnel are prepared to come across to the RSS operation and wear the Royal Signals uniform. For the Gilnahirk operation it all looks very promising although from an item at the next meeting it seems there were still a few bumps to be ironed as simple misunderstanding over promotion had caused a temporary lack of local volunteers.

Senior Officer's Conference Meeting No 25 – Wednesday September 23rd 1942

Mobile direction finding unit mounted on pantechnicon

Item 1.
MOBILE UNITS.
Major Elmes reported the nine Post Office operators at Gilnahirk had now signified their intention of coming over to SCU 3. Mr Hollinghurst stated that he had ascertained that Mr Streeter had not attempted to dissuade men from coming over. The reason why so few men had volunteered was apparently due to a misunderstanding on the question of promotion which had now been cleared up by Major Elmes on his recent visit.

Item 15.
MOVE OF BARNET MOBILE UNIT BASE.
The controller stated that no action could be taken at present on the suggested move of the Barnet Mobile Unit Base to the West Country until after the base at Gilnahirk had been taken over and was running satisfactorily. Major Elmes was instructed to look out for a suitable site in the West Country for a future move.

Senior Officer's Conference Meeting No 26 – Wednesday October 7th 1942

Item 1.
STATION 4
Major Sabine reported that the militarization of station No 4 was satisfactorily accomplished with effect from October 1st, and that no troubles were experienced. A further six operators would be required and arrangements were being made for these to be posted as soon as possible.

Despite all the talk of closure, the Gilnahirk site was retained and renamed as Station No 4, under the control and direction of Special Communications Unit No 3. Taking into consideration the number of additional staff it appears the brick buildings belonging to the Royal Signals unit have been taken over by Station No 4.

Additional note. The Special Communications Units of which there were a number were collectively under the control of MI8c a sub division of Military Intelligence responsible for all signals intelligence gathering.

To complete this section, it is perhaps worthwhile to reflect on the wartime career of Ballygowan man Arthur Irwin who moved from VI to full-time radio operator with the RSS.

Arthur Irwin (GI5TK)

Arthur was born a farmer's son in the townland of Ravara, Ballygowan, County Down. He appears to have been a smart, intelligent young man who from a very early age took a keen interest in wireless telegraphy. His father had presented Arthur with a crystal set and by his early teens Arthur had converted an old pig house on the farm into his radio shack.

In 1934 we have a post card among Arthur's papers which comes from no less a person than Thomas Palmer Allen. TP had himself been interested in wireless telegraphy since as far back as 1927 and may have known Arthur through his attending classes at the Municipal College of Technology Belfast. TP was an instructor of electrical engineering at this college and that subject also included wireless telegraphy. Arthur would have attended these classes to obtain his Post Master General's Certificate which then allowed him to obtain a licence to operate a wireless transmitter.

A reading of the card would suggest that Arthur is very keen to improve his capabilities in relation to wireless telegraphy and TP is suggesting that he consider joining the Royal Naval Wireless Auxiliary Reserve. This will improve his ability to both send and receive Morse coded transmissions, but it will also keep Arthur up to date with all the advances in wireless telegraphy.

top: Arthur Irwin wearing his Naval Uniform
below: Arthur's first radio shack

One assumes Arthur took advantage of this offer for by the time war breaks out Arthur's full-time civilian occupation is as a radio instructor for the merchant marine working at the Caledonian Wireless College in North Street, Belfast training others who will go to sea to join the Royal or Merchant Navy as ships wireless operators. At the same time Arthur maintained his keen interest in amateur radio but along with all those with similar interests he was forced to shut down his broadcasting on the 31st August 1939 although from his log book it would seem he was broadcasting right up to an hour before the deadline.

Atrhur's occupation would have fallen into the category known as a "Reserved Occupation," someone, who if conscription applied would not be called up however he is not exempted from serving in other ways and in July 1940 Arthur receives a letter of invitation from Captain Joe Banham to consider becoming a Voluntary Interceptor. As we already know, Arthur is known through his attendance at the Municipal College Belfast, the Royal Naval Reserve and Amateur radio to TP Allen who I believe may have been the RSGB's regional officer in Northern Ireland when the recruitment process for the RSS began. It was therefore only natural that Arthur's name would be placed before Banham for consideration.

above: Card from TP Allen
below: Arthur's amateur radio log –
note the last entry 'QRT FOR WAR'

By November 1940 Arthur is doing his bit, sending in logs but Banham is requesting that he pay particular attention to the times and frequencies of these wanted stations. Banham also adds this fact. The strength of signal is that heard in the Belfast area. This does not suggest that the signals are emanating from the Belfast area, but they can be heard clearly in the Belfast area. Remember Arthur lives eight miles from Belfast so his reception may be somewhat better. It is also interesting to note that Banham has moved the RSS regional office into the BBC HQ at Linen Hall Street, Belfast. The work of the Post Engineering department is complete and he has moved on. The BBC will have access to both teleprinters and radio transmitter / receivers, so this is a good location for the regional office. One final point I picked up from the letter. The RSS stamp is still showing the word section and not service.

Please note new address :-

REGIONAL OFFICER,
N.I. REGION,
RADIO SECURITY SECTION,
ROOM No. 26,
B.B.C. BUILDING,
31, LINENHALL STREET,
BELFAST.

BELFAST 22323.

67275

9th November, 1940.

Dear Mr. Irwin,

Although we have not heard from you for some little time, I sincerely trust that you have not forgotten us. Your logs were always so interesting - ones that we looked forward to receiving.

I am enclosing herewith list of times and frequencies of wanted stations; these were taken off logs received within the last day or two. The strength shown is that as received in Belfast.

If I can be of any help to you in any way, please let me know.

Trusting we shall have the pleasure of receiving some more of your logs.

Yours sincerely,

J. Banham Captain.
Capt. R. Signals,
Regional Officer, R.S.S.
"N.I." Region.

Mr. A. Irwin,
"Hollyvale",
Ravara,
Ballygowan,
Belfast.

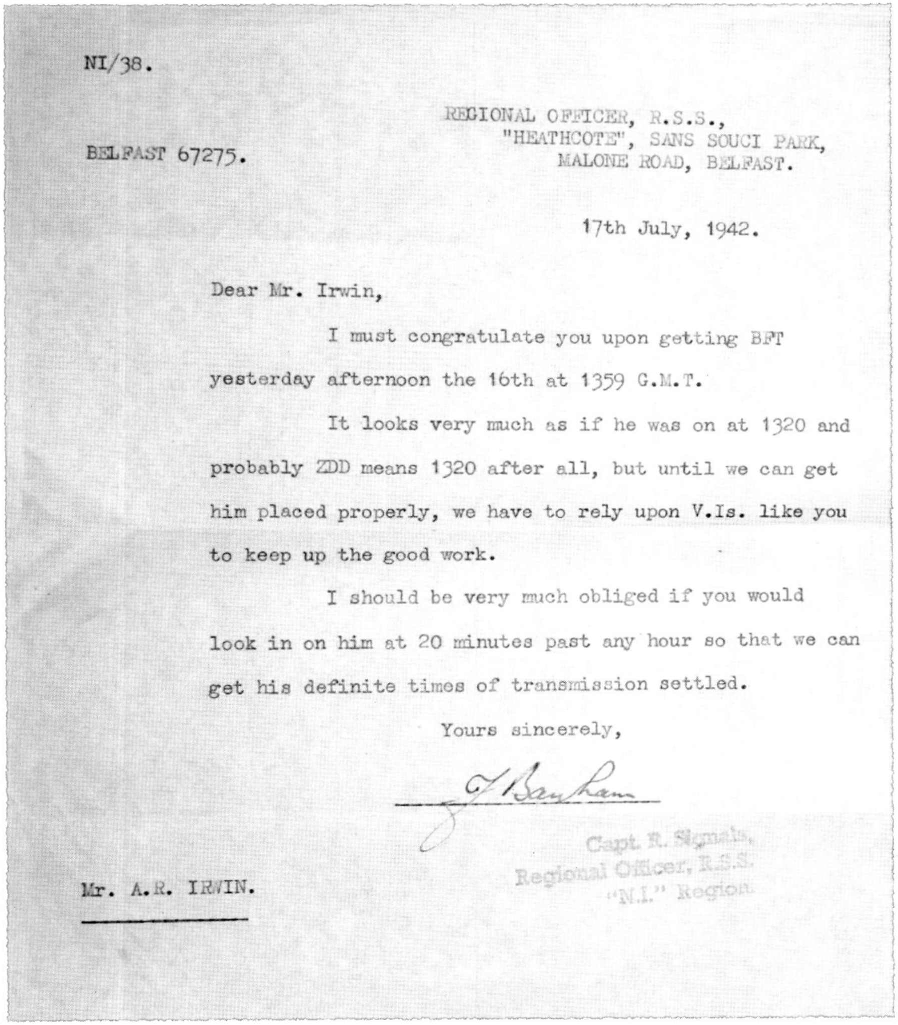

NI/38.

REGIONAL OFFICER, R.S.S.,
"HEATHCOTE", SANS SOUCI PARK,
MALONE ROAD, BELFAST.

BELFAST 67275.

17th July, 1942.

Dear Mr. Irwin,

     I must congratulate you upon getting BFT yesterday afternoon the 16th at 1359 G.M.T.

     It looks very much as if he was on at 1320 and probably ZDD means 1320 after all, but until we can get him placed properly, we have to rely upon V.Is. like you to keep up the good work.

     I should be very much obliged if you would look in on him at 20 minutes past any hour so that we can get his definite times of transmission settled.

     Yours sincerely,

J Bayham

Capt. R. Signals,
Regional Officer, R.S.S.
"N.I." Region.

Mr. A.R. IRWIN.

This letter congratulates Arthur Irwin for the successful detection and interception of something the authorities are keen to understand. Most people overlook the simple fact that without the work of our VIs, the Full-time Operators and the "Y" Service as a whole the men and women at Bletchley Park would have had absolutely nothing to work on during the war.

Letter to Arthur from his parents congratulating him on his appointment to a full-time post with the RSS. "Congratulations on being selected to work along with the stripes and pips, perhaps in your next letter you will have earned a stripe yourself". As the picture of Sergeant Arthur Irwin below shows, their hopes were not long in being fulfilled.

Hollyvale
Ravara
Ballygowan
7.10.42

Dear Arthur

Many thanks for your post card dated 30th Sept. & letter 3rd Oct. received on Monday Tuesday respectively. We were very glad to get them after such a long silence, however we had read one of Meta's & that told us a lot. It and my last one were full of intresting news about yourself. Congratulations on being selected to work along with the stripes & pips, perhaps in your next letter you will have earned a stripe yourself or maybe two !!! Is the work same as you did at home in the or is it experimenting with wire & soldering iron. Mother & I send our compliments to your new cook he sure is a wonder, are you sure he don't boil the tea. Watch you don't get fat with eating so much you won't need any C.L. Oil capsules this winter or Anti-Bi-Son either, well so much the better. You seem to have enough clothes to last you for the duration but if you need some more we could send some along how about your socks have you learned to darn yet or found anyone to do it for you. I saw Aunt Hannah on Tuesday night she asked if we had had any news from Arthur but I need not ask that he will have written to you. I said you had written her but she has not yet received it, nor did Bob & Sophy get the unstamped P.C. according to Meta. She was on the phone on Tues. & I told her about your omission, she saw the C's same day & I suppose asked if they had got one, it had not arrived then

Arthur duly accepts the call to serve King and Country and by the second half of 1940 he is now a working as a VI.

The above letter from Banham in July 1942 shows Arthur is clearly hitting the nail on the head when it comes to seeking out what the RSS wants. Banham is not slow to give credit where credit is due and this goes a long way to explaining what happens next in Arthur's service with the Radio Security Service. This letter also reveals Arthur's Northern Ireland VI number which is thirty-eight (does that indicate there are at least thirty-eight VIs working in Northern Ireland at this time?) and also that Banham has moved the regional office into 'Heathcote' a private house in the Malone area of South Belfast, where it shall remain until the end of the war.

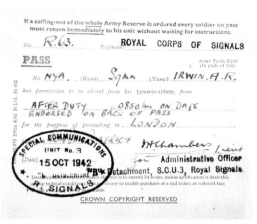

Travel pass dated 15 October 1942 granted to Arthur to travel up to London.

Come 1942 and with the reorganisation of the RSS into a fully military service Arthur's good work is recognised and, having been approached by Captain Banham, Arthur accepts the invitation to become a full-time operator at Station No 4.

In order to comply with this move from VI to full-time operator Arthur required some additional training at Barnet in regards to security procedures etc. and a letter from Arthur to his parents in Ballygowan confirmed he was already training at Barnet on the 30th September 1942.

Having successfully completed his training Arthur returned to N. Ireland and proceeded directly to his new place of employment at Station No 4 (as Gilnahirk was now known) where he served up to and after VE Day.

Long after the war Arthur could be seen in the garden of his home at Crossnacreey wearing his army togs – recycling or a subtle hint at a relationship which had never been broken?

George Browne, himself an amateur radio enthusiast and good friend of Arthur's informed me that, right up to his death, Arthur

Arthur Gardening in Army togs

Arthur Irwin at his radio

annually received a Christmas visit from a gentleman with military connections who presented him with a large bottle of whiskey. Being T-total Arthur passed this on to George.

George said Arthur had a particular interest in working the Russia networks and had established many contacts over the years long after the war and, on the occasion of Arthur's funeral, two well spoken English gentlemen who George believed came from Thiepval barracks Lisburn were in attendance.

I drew from this the possibility that Arthur had continued to listen and report for the security services until he passed away.

When Gilnahirk was established it was to be provided with one Medium Wave Direction Finding Station. One Short Wave Direction Finding Station and twelve intercept positions with a total manpower of fifty-eight GPO civilian personnel. The station like all the others was to be manned twenty-four seven, three hundred and sixty-five days a year with each twenty-four-hour period divided into three watches.

In the diary of Alan Sharpe who was posted to Gilnahirk as the station's maintenance engineer during the month of November 1944 just prior to the official ending of WWII an entry dated 6 May 1945 reveals that a total of fifty-two radio receivers were accounted for at Station No 4 a significant increase over the numbers when the GPO had handed over. So what did they all do?

With the coming of new staff from the mainland Captain Banham had to make arrangements for their accommodation. Crofton Hall a large detached house in the Knock area of East Belfast was requisitioned under the cover of Royal Signals. This became the NAAFI, the Canteen and provided a place where those off duty could relax. Within the grounds a series of Nissan huts were erected to provide off duty accommodation for the various watches. Located close to Knock railway station and the Upper Newtownards Road transport was on hand if you wanted to visit Belfast, Bangor, Newtownards, Donaghadee or further afield.

General Search

First and foremost the function of Gilnahirk was to listen in to the enemy's radio transmissions fulfilling the same function as the VIs only in a more intense and systematic way. Where the VI would man an often low tech radio when he could (nominally 2 hours per day although most did far more) each listening post at Gilnahirk would have been manned constantly using receivers and aerial arrays at the forefront of technology at the time.

Unfortunately I have not been able to source any images of the 'set room' at Gilnahirk but this one of St Erith gives an idea of what the operator positions looked like.

The High Frequency intercept station, the hub of all that took place at Gilnahirk was contained within a long wooden bungalow type building which did not look out of place in the surrounding countryside. In fact its location close to the McDowell family farm would have suggested it may have been nothing more than a hen house from the air. If anything was going to raise suspicions it would have been the collection of telegraph poles that stood proud in the same field and the windows which ran along the length of the bungalow building. However I am told by those who remember this building, that from the Gilnahirk Road it was completely hidden from view. The hedge on top of an embankment, plus a field that was sloping away from the road meant that nothing was visible from a pedestrian's view whilst walking past the site. A clear indication that whoever had placed this building had taken some time to consider its importance and its concealment from unwanted attention.

Access to the building was gained from a gated entrance off the Lisleen Road East. A closed porch with an outer door had been built onto the side of the wooden bungalow which provided a place for coats and hats. The building itself had been divided up into a number of spaces. A small kitchen, toilets, a teleprinter room and the set room. Located around the walls of the set room were the twelve work stations, also known as banks where a trained radio operator would complete his listening watch. A collection of filling cabinets, a couple of tables and some chairs were also provided but that was about it.

Most of the listening positions were 'double banked' ie fitted with two separate receivers which allowed one operator to listen in on two separate transmissions. The first receiver was tuned to the frequency of the sender of the message. The second receiver was tuned to the reply frequency which may be different from the sender. This arrangement allowed the operator to capture both messages. You will note there are two sets of headphones on the table, but each set was split allowing our operator to listen to both receivers at the one time. The other headset would have allowed a second operator to confirm the messages if required.

Double bank listening position

The following explanation of how an operator would use the two radios was given to me by Signalman Ray Wright who explained in a letter.

'You asked about the double receiver positions. This refers to two radio receivers side by side and used by one operator. The headphones were split, that is, in one ear you would hear the signal from one receiver and in the other ear you would hear the signal from the other receiver. This arrangement was used when the operator was copying two stations communicating with each other at different frequencies. This happened when a 'sked'* had been established, that is, when known stations had regular times to get in contact with each other. The RSS operator would be ready with each hand on the tuning dial of each receiver and when contact was made you had to copy what was heard in one ear and then the response heard in the other ear. The two stations often tried to dodge you by making a coded signal and then making a slight change in frequency before sending their messages. You had to be fast and find them again. When they had lots of traffic to send it was the most exhausting work because everything that was sent by both stations had to be written down on pads with carbon paper copies. So before the sked you would charge up a stack of pads with carbon paper, and hope that you had enough to last the time of the transmissions. I remember it well.
Cheers
Ray'

*Over time the RSS built up a picture of the enemy's communications procedures. Under these procedures certain stations would communicate at particular times and particular frequencies which the RSS could predict and these anticipated broadcasts were known as 'skeds'

Due to a myriad of environmental factors which effected their calibration, the frequencies indicated on the dials of the main receivers of the time such as the AR88 or Hallicrafter, were often inaccurate especially in the higher wavebands where errors of 50 kHz were not uncommon. Because functions such as direction finding require an accurate frequency settings the concentrator position was equipped with an expensive frequency meter which could generate a signal at an accurate frequency using a crystal held at a constant temperature in a tiny oven. The operator manning the concentrator position could tune in the signal he wanted to measure on his receiver and then feed in the oscillation produced by his frequency meter until the two signals combined (beat together) to produce a whistle in his earphones. He then moved the fine tuning dial of his frequency meter until the whistle fell off in pitch to below audio level - usually less than 50Hz at which point the frequencies of the two signals would be closely matched. He could then read the dial settings on the frequency meter to get the accurate frequency which he would announce to the net as the true or measured frequency. The intercept operator would then enter that value in his log as the true frequency as opposed to his original reading.

The listening posts were also linked together via a concentrator which consisted of a switching panel and other equipment manned by a skilled operator who use his equipment to link various parts of the listening network both within Gilnahirk or even to the stations on the mainland. This ability to cross link an incoming signal to various stations was vital as I shall explain later when trying to pin down the geographical position of the enemy broadcast stations.

In addition the concentrator contained specialist equipment to make accurate measurements of the enemy's broadcast frequency (see left).

Each bank was manned on a 24 hour basis and even during shift changes there were special procedures to be followed to ensure listening continuity as explained to me by Kenneth Joseph Larkin a Post Office teleprinter operator who worked at Gilnahirk from 1940 until 1942. On occasions Kenneth had the opportunity to witness at first hand the watch changes within the set room.

"The oncoming wireless operator hung up his coat and hat collecting his wireless headset from the same peg. Placing this over his ears he walked towards the receiving bank he was assigned to take over. Plugging into that position he then tapped the sitting operator on the shoulder indicating that he was ready to take over. The coming off watch operator now stood up whilst still recording his log sheet which he had placed on a clip board allowing the oncoming watch operator to sit down. The oncoming operator took a pencil to a new log sheet and started recording. Once the off going watch operator saw that they were both recording the same message he tapped the oncoming watch operator on the shoulder. He then unplugged his wireless headset. The watch had been successfully changed and when both log sheets are compared a small portion of the same message will appear on both log sheets. The continuity of the listening process was maintained and there was no loss of information."

Kenneth went on to say this was all done in a matter of seconds. The watch had been changed, the men had gone for the bus and nothing stirred until the next watch arrived.

If the call of nature came whilst on watch the operator had to seek permission from the duty officer before leaving his work station / bank. Any nourishment in the form of a sandwich, soup or tea was taken at the work station.

The period of a watch may have been divided into various tasks including periods of general searching when the operator has been allocated a given frequency range which he will trawl back and forward recording all Morse coded traffic interspaced with 'Skeds' as described above.

The listening post operators had to be blessed with great powers of concentration. The Germans would often deliberately broadcast in crowded parts of the radio spectrum where their signals would be hard to pick out unless you knew the precise broadcast frequency and the vagaries of ionospheric propagation would mean a signal could be constantly fading in and out. In addition, the Germans would often change frequencies making it difficult to keep locked into a particular transmitter and reducing the value of the intelligence gained.

However, as the war progressed and the operator 'got to know' their adversaries there were several factors which worked in their favour two of which are worth mentioning.

1. Operator's 'fist'

In the same way that different people have different styles of handwriting, the way different radio operators will send Morse code will also vary. Subtle differences in speed, rhythm and accuracy can make the messages they send as distinctive to the experienced listener as if they had hand written them.

As the RSS listeners became familiar with their targets they would be able to recognise each operator's distinctive style known in the world of radio as his 'fist'

Thus should a German radio operator try to make it difficult for anyone listening in to his broadcast by swapping frequencies and call signs etc, a trained listener could still keep track by recognising the senders fist.

2. Radio set 'fingerprint'

In the same way that the radio operators were distinctive, so the radio sets of the time also had their distinctive idiosyncrasies often sending out extraneous signals which could be picked up and analysed thus identifying the particular transmitter being used.

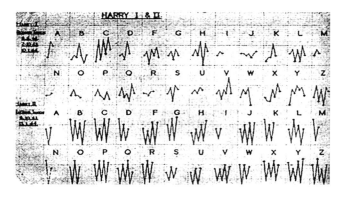

Examples of radio set fingerprint of the Abwher networks Harry one and two

This was achieved by taking a photograph of the signal trace from an oscilloscope. Each trace was like a fingerprint and by comparing oscilloscope photographs it was possible to recognise that two or more transmissions sent on different frequencies by different operators were in fact coming from the same German radio transmitter.

Information like this forms part of what today would be called the meta-data of the message ie that information which could be deduced from the message without actually cracking the cipher and reading its contents.

All this data along with the message itself including its preamble (the first part of the message stating who it was for and who it was from) would be recorded on the pads Ray refers to in his letter which are broadly the same as used by the VIs for recording the messages they picked up ready for the next stage of the process, discrimination.

As previously explained, due to the vagaries of shortwave radio, transmissions by German radio stations may be heard by a listener in one location but not by his fellow listener in the next county or different parts of the same message might be picked up by two different listeners as atmospheric conditions changed altering how the signal propagated. However by having a large number of listeners spread throughout the UK there was a good chance that between them all the complete message would be picked up even if it was a bit here, a snippet there and another part elsewhere. The discrimination procedure was designed to bring all these loose ends together into one complete picture.

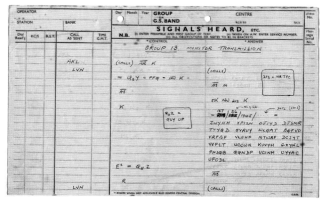

Log sheet

The first step of the procedure was to gather all the information on the radio log sheets being produced by both the full-time and part time operators of the listening process in one place at the RSS headquarters.

In the beginning this had been located at Wormwood Scrubs prison but, come the Blitz on London, a safer location was required and the RSS began a process of looking for a new home. Eventually a suitable site was found in the village of Barnet approximately fifty miles from London. It ticked all the boxes and very quickly work began to convert and make ready the site which consisted of a large house known locally as 'Arkley View' sitting within its own grounds which had the potential to meet the needs of the RSS for the foreseeable future. A series of large wooden huts were erected not unlike the bungalow type building at Gilnahirk and it was these huts which were the destination of mail sent to the mysterious PO Box 25, Barnet.

Construction begins at Arkley view

Each day hundreds and hundreds of radio log sheets arrived from all over the British Isles to be systematically sorted by first date, then time and finally the radio frequency they were picked up on.

This simple sorting procedure results in multiple files of log sheets each file consisting of multiple copies of the same transmission. i.e. Each log sheet is a recording of the same incoming Morse coded message recorded at various locations across the British Isles.

For each file a master log sheet is drawn up and using a pencil an exact copy of the first recording is made on the master log sheet. This is then compared with the next log sheet in the file, discrepancies are noted (eg a different letter in a given position) blanks filled in etc until, by the time all the log sheets have been processed, a true and full copy of the original message should be obtained. With the process complete the master and all the copies are tied together.

Log sheets being sorted at Arkley

But even before the intercepted messages were passed to the code breakers just down the road at Bletchley Park there was more information which could be gleaned from them using the techniques of traffic analysis as developed by the outstanding mathematician and early recruit to the Bletchley operation, Gordon Welchman.

By examining all the meta data for each signal (such as the preamble, the message origination, message destination, time/date information and so on) and methodically recording it all on a database which could be analysed using various techniques developed by Gordon Welchman and others, over time a picture emerges of the enemy's activity. Who is speaking to whom and why, where the command centres are and what they are commanding, changes in operational tempo such as may precede an operation – the potential intelligence which can be garnered from such analysis is remarkable without ever breaking and reading a single encrypted radio signal.

Of course as the experts at Arkley and Bletchley Park gradually pried open Germany's secrets they could see that intercepted signals from certain sources were more valuable than others showing what the intelligence gathering operation needed to focus on.

To get this information back to the operators actually sitting at the radio sets the radio log sheets, after every available scrap of information on them had been recorded were marked up and sent back to the operators.

Careful procedures were in place to ensure that after the operators and VIs had seen them, the marked up log sheets would be destroyed to avoid any potential security breaches. In N. Ireland it seems that Capt. Joe Banham paid regular visits to the homes of his VIs where he collected the returned logs sheets and then burned them leaving no evidence for posterity. As such I was delighted to discover during a meeting with Pamela Allen, TP Allen's daughter, that she still had in her position some 26 of her father's log sheets (I don't know how they slipped through the security net) which clearly show the sort of information being passed backwards and forwards.

On the following pages I have included a selection of these log sheets to illustrate what I like to call the bread and butter of the whole listening process, namely the two way flow of information between those gathering and those analysing. The log sheets show how the British intelligence machine is constantly adjusting and refining its radio listening operations to target the key areas of the German war effort. Given that by 1941 Arkley was processing some 10000 of these sheets per day the scale of the operation and its ability to unearth information vital to the allied war effort is clear.

This data sheet dated 4 June 1942 has two entries which have been ticked by the analysts at Barnet. The colour is green and this indicates the subjects have been successfully covered. One is timed at 18:30hrs the other 19:30hrs. The first entry timed at 18:00hrs and 18:15hrs has drawn a blank and those at Barnet are suggesting he look for this transmission again at 13650 or 14500.

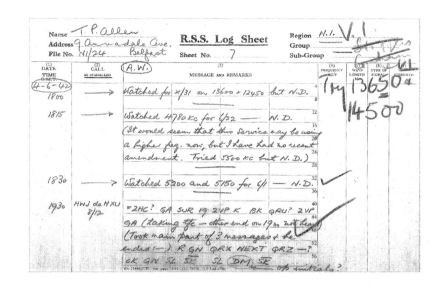

R.S.S. Log Sheet

Name	T. P. Allen		Region	N.I.
Address	9 Annadale Ave. Belfast		Group	
File No.	N1/24	Sheet No. 7	Sub-Group	

(1) DATE TIME G.M.T.	(2) CALL AS SIGNALLED	(3) MESSAGE and REMARKS	(4) FREQUENCY Kc/S	(5) WAVE LENGTH	(6) TYPE OF SIGNAL	STRENGTH
4-6-42	A.W.					
1800	→	Watched for X/31 on 13600 + 12450 but N.D.	Try 13650 14500			
1815	→	Watched 4780 Kc for 4/22 — N.D. (It would seem that this Service may be using a higher freq. now, but I have had no recent amendment. Tried 5500 Kc but N.D.)				
1830	→	Watched 5200 and 5150 for 4/1 — N.D. ✓				
1930	HWJ de HXU 8/12	=ZHC? GA SUR 19 2VIP K BK QRU? 2VIP GA (taking tfc — other end on 19m not heard (Took main part of 3 messages + he ended —) R GN QRX NEXT QRZ —? OK GN SL SL SL DM SE				

This document informed TP Allen that his log sheet dated 12 May 1942 has been kept. This log sheet contained something of interest to those at Barnet. It was most unlikely that any further detail will be revealed about the contents of this log to TP Allen.

V.I. T. P. Allen NI/24 V

Your log dated 12.5.42 .... containing the following particulars has been kept.

Particulars: Call CDE on 12500 kc/s at 1800 GMT

PBL: NW W50 37 3459 = 00242 = 5LC

Other details: ....

....

If A.W.Log: This is not the Service allocated to you, it is already covered elsewhere.
Remarks: ....
....

If G.S.Log: G.S.Band........kc/s to............kc/s.
1. Identified and covered, thank you.
2. Suspect. Please report again when heard.

Special remarks: Heard while standing by x/31 — not X/31 on but a SUSPECT
....
....

83

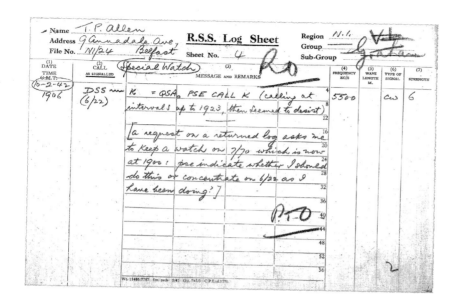

Name T.P. Allen
Address 9 Annadale Ave, Belfast
File No. N1/24
R.S.S. Log Sheet
Region N.I.
Group
Sub-Group
Sheet No. 4

DATE TIME G.M.T.	CALL AS SIGNALLED	MESSAGE and REMARKS	FREQUENCY KC/S	WAVE LENGTH M.	TYPE OF SIGNAL	STRENGTH
10-2-42 1906	DSS (6/22)	K = QSA₂ PSE CALL K (calling at intervals up to 1923, then seemed to desist)	5500		Cw	6
		[a request on a returned log asks me to keep a watch on 7/70 which is now at 1900: pse indicate whether I should do this or concentrate on 6/22 as I have been doing?]				
		P.T.O				

This log sheet dated 10 February 1942 contains a message from TP seeking guidance on which direction he is to follow. The reply has been written on the reverse of this log sheet and returned to him. The reply gives a number of different frequencies and suggests it may be better to search for the suspect in the evenings.

The following five sheets comprise the complete log submitted by TP Allen for a single signal he picked up on 26 January 1942.

Name T.P. Allen
Address 9 Annadale Ave, Belfast
File No. N1/24
R.S.S. Log Sheet
Region N.I.
Group
Sub-Group
Sheet No. 1

Special Watch

DATE TIME G.M.T.	CALL AS SIGNALLED	MESSAGE and REMARKS	FREQUENCY KC/S	WAVE LENGTH M.	TYPE OF SIGNAL	STRENGTH
26-1-42 1910	DMN (6/22)	ER QSA₂ ER NIL TKS DR OM GB CUL= SK (QRM from very strong signal calling "16P" repeatedly, then "K", at about 1½ w.p.m.)	5500		Cw	5
1915		Watch for 7/70 on 3870 but N.D.				
1930		Went on watch for 2/355 but was lured into copying LPR (reported on separate sheet). He did not give c/s until later. Would you please identify this LPR merchant for me — I cannot place him on what schedules I possess. Thanking you T.P.				

Thank you.

Now up at 1900, and reply apparently using c/s. Will you kindly watch & report anything suspicious o.m.? 735 TW.

LPR is Rep'd service 3/15 Willie Sked

84

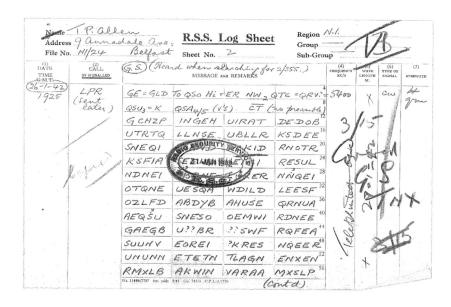

Name: T. P. Allen
Address: 9 Annadale Ave, Belfast
File No. N1/24

R.S.S. Log Sheet

Sheet No. 2

Region N.1.
Group
Sub-Group

(1) DATE TIME G.M.T.	(2) CALL AS SIGNALLED	(3) (G.S.) (Heard when searching for 2/355.) MESSAGE and REMARKS				(4) FREQUENCY KC/S	(5) WAVE LENGTH M.	(6) TYPE OF SIGNAL	(7) STRENGTH
26-1-42 1925 (sent later)	LPR	GE = GLD To QSO Hi = ER NW, QTC = QRV? =				5400	X	CW	4 gru
		QSU₃ = K	QSA4/5 (V's)	CT (no preamble)					
		G CHZP	INGEH	UIRAT	DEDOB				
		UTRTQ	LLNSE	UBLLR	KSDEE				
		SNEQI	... KID	RNOTR					
		KSFIA	...	RESUL					
		NDNEI	... ER	NNQEI					
		OTQNE	UESQA	WDILD	LEESF				
		OZLFD	ABDYB	AHUSE	QRNUA				
		AEQSU	SNESO	OEMWI	RDNEE				
		GAEGB	U??BR	??SWF	RQFEA				
		SUUNV	EOREI	?KRES	NQEER				
		UNUNN	ETETN	TLAGN	ENXEN				
		RMXLB	AKWIN	VARAA	MXSLP				

Wt. 11486/7787 6m. pads 5/41 Gp. 745/1 C.P.Ltd.1770.

(Cont'd.)

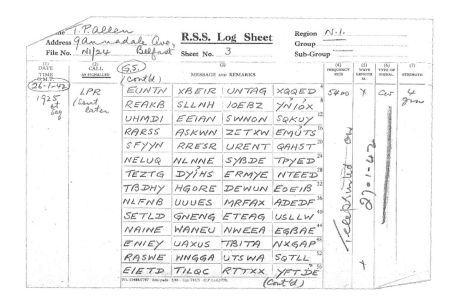

Name: T. P. Allen
Address: 9 Annadale Ave, Belfast
File No. N1/24

R.S.S. Log Sheet

Sheet No. 3

Region N.1.
Group
Sub-Group

(1) DATE TIME G.M.T.	(2) CALL AS SIGNALLED	(3) (G.S.) (Cont'd) MESSAGE and REMARKS				(4) FREQUENCY KC/S	(5) WAVE LENGTH M.	(6) TYPE OF SIGNAL	(7) STRENGTH
26-1-42 1925 et seq	LPR (sent later)	EUNTN	XBEIR	UNTAG	XQQED	5400	X	CW	4 gru
		REAKB	SLLNH	IOEBZ	YNIOX				
		UHMDI	EEIAN	SWNON	SQKUY				
		RARSS	ASKWN	ZETXW	EMUTS				
		SFYYN	RRESR	URENT	QAHST				
		NELUQ	NLNNE	SYBDE	TPYED				
		TEZTG	DYIHS	ERMYE	NTEED				
		TBDHY	HGORE	DEWUN	EOEIB				
		NLFNB	UUUES	MRFAX	ADEDF				
		SETLD	GNENG	ETEAG	USLLW				
		NAINE	WANEU	NWEEA	EGBAE				
		ENIEY	UAXUS	TBITA	NXGAP				
		RASWE	WNGGA	UTSWA	SQTLL				
		EIETD	TILQC	RTTXX	YFTDE				

Wt. 11486/7787 6m. pads 5/41 Gp. 745/1 C.P.Ltd.1770.

(Cont'd)

Sheet 4

Name T.P. Allen
Address 9 Annadale Ave, Belfast
File No. N1/24

R.S.S. Log Sheet

Sheet No. 4

Region N.I.
Group
Sub-Group

(1) DATE TIME G.M.T.	(2) CALL AS SIGNALLED	(G.S) (contd) (3) MESSAGE AND REMARKS				(4) FREQUENCY KC/S	(5) WAVE LENGTH M.	(6) TYPE OF SIGNAL	(7) STRENGTH
26-1-42 1925 et seq	LPR (sent later)	LXIDL	QQNTO	TUEWS	NINHI [4]	5400	X	cw	4 gm
		??XXB	SGESE	DMSLY	SEYLM [8]				
		SVEEU	NF?KE	RENNG	FTLBG [12]				
		SQQLG	ESIOT	KEWJE	EUTBR [16]				
		HETNR	TMNE?	NIEIG	??MAY [20]				
		KFTEF	EDUBG	R̃ENDN	ESNOB [24]				
		DRORE	BTVNA	RXSAZ	FADRU [28]				
		TIUDU	UGXNA	ENAYN	UUAKS [32]				
		FGOMW	AARNX	YINAT	TNAA? [36]				
		TDID?	GUBNG	LMDTO	GWIAL [40]				
		RREAA	EIEME(?)	XPW +	A̅S̅ [44]				
		UR QTC	Q2J	ES OK	A̅S̅₂ (then [48]				
		a second message followed as [52]							
		reported on next sheet) [56]							

(vertical note: Telephoned on 27-1-42)

Wt. 11486/7787 6m. pads 5/41 Gp. 745/3 C.P.Ltd.1770.

Sheet 5

Name T.P. Allen
Address 9 Annadale Ave,
File No. N1/24   Belfast

R.S.S. Log Sheet

Sheet No. 5

Region N.I.
Group
Sub-Group

(1) DATE TIME G.M.T.	(2) CALL AS SIGNALLED	(G.S.) (3) MESSAGE AND REMARKS C̅T̅				(4) FREQUENCY KC/S	(5) WAVE LENGTH M.	(6) TYPE OF SIGNAL	(7) STRENGTH
26-1-42 1925	LPR (sent later)	OFIMA	ZEERA	GN?NW	R???N [4]	5400	X	cw	4 gm gm
		ELEUS	RTADG	TNDOE	LRREF [8]				
		UNEER	EHTDC	TAREQ	NEYFN [12]				
		NRRAX	OEFRU	D2INL	DESRU [16]				
		KEEDF	XEASS	QUEME	SREKE [20]				
		LRTKQ	AUNIO	RLROX	NTUYN [24]				
		YEDON	MENDS	LN2IF	RNMSU [28]				
		AAPHL	EFANI	NHSTQ	NLEZE [32]				
		EDEE	+ A̅S̅	GLD =	FB= [36]				
		QSO =	73 ES GN	R QSU₂ = GA	R [40]				
		QS̃A₄	8/9	R TKS 73 ES GB	+ S̅K̅ [44]				
		[48]							
		[52]							
		[56]							

(vertical note: Telephoned on 27-1-42)

Wt. 11486/7787 6m. pads 5/41 Gp. 745/3 C.P.Ltd.1770.

Teleprinter Room

Towards the end of their time running Gilnahirk the GPO had three teleprinter operators on loan to the station and while all the log sheets from N. Ireland were physically sent to Arkley it seems clear that they first went to the teleprinter room at Gilnahirk from where they were sent electronically by land line to Barnet avoiding any delay in passing on vital signals intelligence while the physical copies were transported across the Irish sea.

Manning one of these teleprinters was Kenneth Joseph Larkin the only living GPO veteran that I met during my ten years of research. Kenneth recalled:

Among a number of wartime photographs taken by signalman Alan Sharpe is one of the teleprinter room at Gilnahirk. The three teleprinters are clear to see and the small electric fire against the far wall would suggest the day is cold outside.

> "My work was constant, never ending and I and my other two colleagues had little time for a breather. We were located in a small room with a window next to the large set room. A small hatch was built into the wall which allowed the completed logs to be passed through to us from the set room. The sliding hatch door was kept closed at all times as the mechanical clatter of the teleprinter was considered a disturbance to the radio operators sitting close to this hatch if it were left open. Tea was served on the hour ever hour and such was the punctuality you could almost set your watch by it."

According to Kenneth the teleprinters were continually sending and receiving information from a central control but when asked where that was Kenneth said he could not remember but then added *"I did not know"* and mentioned without prompting that you very quickly learnt not to ask questions about things that did not concern you.

Given that even the teleprinter operators did not know who they were sending the data to it is interesting to consider how much the VIs and the operators at Gilnahirk would have known about what went on at the mysterious PO Box 25. Had they any idea about what use the constant stream of intercepts they produced were being put? Did they have any inkling as to who was sending or receiving the signals they were monitoring or did they even know who had marked up the log sheets they had dutifully prepared and for what reason?

The answer to all the above is probably no. While the full timers at Gilnahirk would undoubtedly have known a little bit more than the VIs, the whole of the British signals intelligence operation was run on a strictly need to know basis to the extent that I believe that many of the VIs operating in Belfast may not even have known of the existence of the radio station at Gilnahirk.

When questioned about the content of his work Kenneth Larkin had absolutely no recall. *"You were encouraged not to ask questions and I was young and not really interested. It was a job, which I enjoyed, but have few detailed memories apart from what I have told you".*

Despite his response I just had to ask Kenneth what he knew about Bletchley Park. His responses were blunt and to the point which surprised me as I first assumed he was keeping the secret so to speak, but it some became clear he was in no mood for my comments.

"Bletchley, that place where they did all the code breaking during the war. We had nothing to do with that place, don't be stupid?"

You could say things went from bad too worse when I suggested he was entitled to the Bletchley Park Badge which had been announced by the government in 2009. I was shown the door and told politely to go. I recall his final words on the subject, *"My work at Gilnahirk had nothing to do with Bletchley Park."*

Thankfully his wife and daughter who were both present took a more conciliatory approach as I made my way towards the front door. They provided me with a telephone number which I was asked to ring later that evening. Having completed the necessary paperwork on Kenneth's behalf he received his long overdue gold plated Bletchley badge and certificate from the prime minister David Cameron three days later. We often wonder how ten thousand people at Bletchley Park kept a secret for so long after the war, but I believe the answer can be found in Kenneth Larkin's example of an individual working at Gilnahirk who as Asa Briggs said 'belonged to the same Bletchley complex' but was told absolutely nothing regarding the content of his work.

Kenneth passed away in 2015, but for the last four years of his life he could tell his grandchildren and his family and friends of his contribution to the work of Bletchley Park during those first two years of the war.

Mr and Mrs Kenneth Larkin with Kenneth proudly wearing his Bletchley Park badge

I have enjoyed these many years of research. I have met many individuals and I have heard many stories, but nothing gave me more pleasure than revealing to Kenneth the truth behind his wartime service with the Post Office at Gilnahirk Wireless Station.

I unearthed supporting evidence from the archives at BT in the minutes of an S.C.U meeting for Kenneth Larkin's comments on the work load of the teleprinter section

Meeting No 14 Tuesday 3rd February 1942
Item No 9 on the agenda.
GILNAHIRK TELEPRINTER LINE
It was reported that the N.I. Regional Officer was using the Gilnahirk T/P line for transmitting V.I. Logs and Major Morton-Evans said that this was causing delay in the transmission of logs from Gilnahirk station. It was decided that Major Morton-Evans and Major Sabine should go into the matter together and arrange the priority of messages to be sent by Teleprinter.

Meeting No 15 Tuesday 17th February 1942
Item No 10 on the agenda
GILNAHIRK TELEPRINTER LINE
"Major Sabine reported that he had seen Capt., Banham who was settling the matter with Mr Streeter on his return to Gilnahirk as to the question of priority messages."

Direction Finding (D/F)

Once a new enemy transmission source had been picked up by either the full-time listeners or the VIs as previously explained it was important to gather as much information as possible about it and one of the key things to find out was the where in Europe the new transmitter was located.

The operators of the direction finding equipment worked in a metal tank buried underground to shield their equipment from interference from extraneous radio signals. Although not at Gilnahirk, this partially buried tank is the same as that installed at Gilnahirk.

To achieve this Gilnahirk, like the other RSS stations was equipped with a Marconi Adcock Direction Finding (D/F) Installation. This installation consisted of four 10m tall interlinked antenna connected to an underground (to shield it from unwanted radio signals) cabin containing the actual direction finding equipment.

At Gilnahirk Jimmy Mann a near neighbour of the station recalled to me the excavation of a large amount of earth in one field some three hundred yards from the wireless station bungalow. Into this excavation was placed this large metal tank containing the Marconi Adcock Direction Finding Apparatus. This was known as the Underground Cabin. A fair amount of earth was then restored to its former location and after a small amount of landscaping and the application of some grass seed, all appeared normal. Buried just below the surface of the ground, access to the underground cabin was gained through a sliding hatch and some metal steps. On the surface, unless you were standing right at the cabin all you would have seen were four thirty foot wooden telegraph poles rising into the heavens.

But back to the tank. It was about ten feet tall by twelve feet across and inside there was a large table, two chairs, plus an electric fire. Built into the base was a water sump with an electric pump to remove any water which could gather and threaten the safety of the operators working with the high voltage equipment in the tank – cramped but comfortable would have been a good way to describe conditions.

Over the years rumours have abounded that what you could see on the surface of the main postwar building was only part of the wireless station. Some individuals suggested there was even more below the surface but I can confirm the Marconi Adcock underground cabin was the only aspect of the Gilnahirk site that was buried below the ground.

I shall not go into the technical detail of how the Marconi Adcock direction finding system worked but suffice to say it allows the operator in the underground cabin to find the compass bearing of an enemy transmitter he had tuned into.

Operator using the D/F equipment

To have an overview of how D/F was used let us assume that a signal from an unidentified source has been picked up by a VI or one of the full-time listeners and headquarters staff want to know from whence it came. The frequency will have been recorded by the operator who intercepted the signal in the first place and HQ in Barnet now alerts all our full-time listening stations to be on stand by for the next time any transmission is heard on this frequency.

All over the country one operator in each of the listening stations will monitor this frequency waiting patiently for a transmission. The first to hear that transmission, be he in England, Scotland or Northern Ireland will begin a process using the station concentrator to send that incoming German radio signal down a land line to the Barnet control. Once that signal is heard at the Barnet control it is immediately passed out to the Direction Finding stations in our RSS network over the RSS private land line network.

Robin Morrow whose father owned the land into which the Underground Cabin was buried, told me a story about how he got to look into the underground cabin during the War. One night there was a heavy fog over the Castlereagh Hills and out of the mist the lone army guard protecting the Underground Cabin was confronted with the sound of movement and breathing. In the mist he could see nothing so issued a challenge in the normal military manner. "Who goes there?" but gets no reply. Again the challenge is issued and once again there is no reply. The nerves of the guard are on edge and after a third and final challenge he fires a single round from his rifle. A thump is heard and all goes quiet. By this stage the alarm has been raised and other guards arrive to help and conduct a quick search revealing a freshly shot dead cow a short distance from the D/F site! Soon other cows are seen through the mist wandering around the D/F site and a call is made to Robin's father to come and round up his animals and he and Robin soon had the remaining animals returned to their proper field. Making their way back to the family farm the pair were passing close to the D/F site when suddenly and without warning one of the D/F/ operators slides back the access cover to the underground cabin and climbs out like a ghost rising from the grave causing a very young and extremely frightened Robin Morrow to start screaming his head off. After getting Robin settled, his father explains all and takes him over to see where the D/F operator had come from. Peering down into the tank he can see another operator in the gloom of the red light. Rising up from the tank is a shaft of hot air enriched with

Now, all at the same time, in all the connected D/F stations the D/F operators are hearing the same incoming radio signal being monitored by the full-time operator who first captured it and is now working to stay tuned in to it.

Listening to the signal arriving by landline from Barnet through one of the two ear pieces on his headset, each D/F operator will now tune his own radio receiver within the underground cabin until he hears the same signal in the other earpiece of his headset confirming he has captured the same incoming signal.

Having locked on to the signal the D/F operator then uses his direction finding equipment to quickly measure the compass bearing of the incoming signal being picked up by the four 30ft aerials standing proud above the underground cabin.

He passes this bearing back to the Barnet control and so long as at least one other station has got a bearing to the source of the signal it is a simple matter of plotting these bearings on a map to find the position of the transmitter, the accuracy of this position improving if more stations have been able to get a bearing.

The whole of the D/F process only works when the German transmission is on air. Once that transmission stops the D/F process stops with it, no German Signal, no D/F Measurement. However, although it sounds a complex procedure, with trained operators the whole operation could happen remarkably quickly and as the War progresses the RSS were able to build up a detailed picture of the German intelligence operations.

Mobile Search

In addition to the fixed D/F station there were also a number of mobile units attached to the GPO / Military Illicit Wireless Intercept operation at Gilnahirk which would been used to try and pinpoint illegal transmission detected within the province or just across the border. The mobile units would be sent to a general area as a result of a D/F triangulation by the main D/F sites or the detection of a ground wave signal by a Voluntary Interceptor.

If the time and frequency of the transmission were known a joint operation consisting of three or four vehicles which would have moved into an area about one to two hundred yards from the target. Once the transmission started it was just a question of getting good bearings on the signal which could then be triangulated to narrow the search to an individual building.

Personal Memories

The preceding information to the best of my knowledge and based on my research is an explanation of the work that went on at Gilnahirk during the dark days of WWII but what was it like to work there?

For some insight may I refer you to accounts from two people who were involved with Gilnahirk towards the end of the War.

Ray Wright who currently lives in New Zealand is, as far as I can find, the only known living Royal Signals veteran who worked at Gilnahirk after the site became Station No 4 and sent me his recollections of his time with the RSS from which I have extracted the following.

With the ambition of joining the Merchant Navy to serve as a Radio Officer, Ray Wright was a student at the Cardiff Wireless College when Principal approached him to ask if he would be interested in another line of work.

Ray takes up the story;

> "The Principal told me very little of what the work was except that I had to have a certain standard of skill in Morse, which I already acquired. The remuneration was attractive too, so I discussed it with my father. Mindful of the dangers at sea during the war, and the stories told by my cousin who was an engineering officer in the Merchant

cont...

the smell of hot glass radio valves and with Robin's mind at ease, father and son return to the family farm.

Robin's story gives an interesting insight into the security at the site at the time. Those who can remember the wartime site tell me that movement along the Gilnahirk and Lisleen Road East was never restricted by road blocks. It would appear that the military guard remained close to the individual buildings they had been assigned to protect. No unnecessary attention was drawn to the site and I believe that is one reason why it remained so anonymous throughout its working life. One neighbour of the station stated clearly that you rarely if ever saw anyone moving about outside, the change of a watch being conducted in such a way that a period of external activity was over in just a few minutes. Surprisingly there were no fences, no barbed wire and at night the place was in total darkness because of the black out. Guards were rarely seen but, as the Morrow's cow found to its cost, approach any of the buildings associated with some aspect of the station site and someone was out to challenge you immediately.

Navy when he came home on leave, my father raised no opposition to my taking up this mysterious job. The next thing that happened was I had to fill out various forms that required a lot of details about my parents and grandparents and other things. I now know that this was part of the process of Positive Vetting for my security clearance but at the time all I knew was that I then received what I can only describe as a charming letter from my new employers inviting me to come to Arkley"

HM GOVERNMENT COMMUNICATIONS CENTRE (Dept. B)
PO BOX 25, BARNET, HERTS.
16 December, 1944.
R.R. Wright Esq.,
127 Cardiff Road,
Taffs Well,
Glam.

Dear Sir,

   With reference to your application for enlistment into this Unit, we are now prepared to make you the following offer. If accepted, your commencing rate of pay will be £3.10s per week, rising to £5. £6. and £7. According to your qualifications. In addition, you will receive free food, accommodation and uniform. This information is confidential and must not be divulged to any third party.

   If you wish to take advantage of this offer, we shall be glad of confirmation that you will report for training at Barnet on Wednesday the 20th December, 1944. If after examination, you are found to be suitable we will ask the authorities to arrange your enlistment.

   Our address is 'Arkley View', Arkley, Barnet, Herts., and the best way to get here from London is by Northern Line Tube to High Barnet Station. Outside the Station cross the road and a bus on either the Boreham Wood or Watford route will bring you to Arkley Lane; the first house past the lane on the right-hand side of the road is 'Arkley View'.

   You should arrange to arrive as early in the day as train services permit, bringing with you your Identity Card, National Health and Unemployment Insurance Cards or, if an Established Civil Servant, TC 13/39 (from A to be completed by the Head of your department) NS 2 and Medical Grading Cards, all ration books and coupons and as several weeks will elapse before we can arrange enlistment, sufficient civilian clothing to last you over that period. If you are subject to the PAYE Income Tax scheme you should obtain from your present employer and bring with you Parts 2 and 3 of Income Tax form P45. Before leaving your area, you should report to the Allocation Officer, Ministry of Labour, informing him that you wish to proceed to Barnet for the purpose of voluntary enlistment into the Royal Signals and requesting him to forward Form NS 152 (Clearance) to the Departmental Officer, Allocation Office, Ministry of Labour and National Service, St. Albans, Herts.

   You should travel by third-class single ticket, for which you will be reimbursed in due course.
Yours faithfully
Lt. R. Sussex.

Initial training at Arkley (mostly improving their Morse skills) lasted some three months and by March the new recruits had all reached the required standard in Morse and were being gradually introduced into the purpose for which they had been recruited. They were told about interception, frequencies, familiarisation with sets, schedules, (skeds) and international ham chat.

Ray again takes up the story;

Ray Wright

"It was now time for us to be allocated proper duties. We were all to be farmed out to earn our keep. We were scattered far and wide. It is purely supposition on my part but I have long since held the view that new lads like myself were largely being taken on with an eye on the future where many of the older members would be stood down after the war and operators would be needed for a civilianised service. The intercept operating positions were mostly filled with men who had been doing the job for several years.

Initially I spent a few weeks in Arkley doing a basic clerical job in the traffic section before being told that I was to be posted to Gilnahirk. When I found out where Gilnahirk was I was quite pleased, it meant crossing the Irish sea and was almost like an overseas posting.

I left Arkley in April 1945 and said goodbye to all my colleagues in the hut who had yet to receive their posting. And made my way to London to take the train to Scotland, eventually finding my way to Stranraer. I went by ship from Stranraer to Larne in Northern Ireland and as the war was still in progress we had a Royal Navy escort. All this sounds simple but for an 18 years old in those days it was a great adventure and not quite straightforward as the description would indicate. Nevertheless I arrived and took a train from Larne to Belfast where I was to be picked up by a truck and taken to Knock. While waiting for the truck I found a canteen in the railway station which was run by the Catholic Women's Mission, this is where I experienced the first of many sets of Irish hospitality. When I walked in the door I was given a warm welcome by some very motherly ladies who gave me a glass of milk and some cakes. Having come from that part of the UK where just about everything was rationed and in short supply I was slightly overwhelmed. I was to be even more surprised as the weeks passed on just how lightly this place was affected by the tight controls that I had experienced in England.

The truck eventually arrived and I reported into the camp administration office which was an old country house in Barnett's Road with the name of Crofton Hall. The grounds had a high wire fence around the perimeter and a number of nissen huts were located near the house. In the office I was welcomed by a very friendly young Lieutenant who was kind enough to enquire if I had a good crossing. I was taken to one of the nissen huts and shown where I was to sleep, then introduced to the other facilities the camp had to offer, such as the mess room and the canteen. I was given a day to settle in and then taken to where the work was done, the intercept station at Gilnahirk. I was given patches to sew on to the sleeves of my battledress tunic. I was never to discover the full meaning of them but troops based in Northern Ireland seemed to wear them. They comprised of a rectangle of green with a white farm gate embroidered on it. I was warned to avoid the Falls Road area of Belfast as this was strictly off limits to all military personnel working at Gilnahirk. The station was manned 24 hours a day and staffed by three shifts. As far as I can recall the shifts were from 7am to 3pm, 3pm to 11pm, and the night shift was 11pm to 7am. A separate nissen hut at Crofton hall provided a quiet place to sleep for those coming off night duty if your own hut had members who were off duty and up and about.

The truck ride from Knock to Gilnahirk was quite short and could be walked if one liked exercise and a hike. The station, comprising of a long low shed-like structure set in open country. It would be assumed to be connected with farming, rather than a secret radio establishment. Inside there were banks of radio receivers along each wall in the receiving room. A supervisor's desk was placed in the centre at one end. Other rooms included a small office where there was an over line communications apparatus with Morse key etc. In addition, there were the usual facilities of toilet and kitchen. Now searching my memory and trying to conjure up mental pictures of the layout I have always believed that there was a teleprinter room at the station, now I am not sure, possibility it was at Knock at Crofton Hall. Similarly, there has recent mention of a direction finding facility at Gilnahirk. I can only say that I never saw or heard of any such facility. If there had been one, I would probably have met the operators if they lived in the camp. It is also a subject that has interested me for many years so I think I would have remembered if there was one at Gilnahirk.

On my first day on shift I was informed that my main job was to maintain the land line link. All the intercept operator positions have been filled largely by long serving men, some of whom lived locally. Never the less they were all in uniform. So my main job was to send and receive messages via the on-line Morse link while others did the more challenging jobs of meeting 'Skeds' i.e. intercepting enemy traffic. I had no certain way of knowing where the traffic came from but it was generally believed to between units of the German armed forces. At that stage the war in Europe was all but over and the importance of this category of intercept must have started to wane. I have no idea of the where the change of area interest was to be directed but presumably there would be one and based on the location of Gilnahirk it was still likely to have been somewhere in Europe.

The personnel at Gilnahirk are worthy of comment. In my view there were three categories. Firstly, there were a handful of young men who had come through the system at Arkley. They seem to have the lesser jobs, like the one I had, whilst others were detailed to operate the teleprinters and the like. Some of the ones who had come much earlier did have intercept work but it seemed that I had arrived at a time when they did not really need any more staff. Never the less, one like myself could have been less than awe struck at the importance of the work that was being done and proud to be a very small cog in this vital machine.

Then there were the old RSS hands some of whom had been involved in the communications business all their lives, either professional telegraphists or as radio amateurs. They were very skilled and it was right and proper that they should hold these jobs. Their contribution to the war effort and their peers at other stations must have been enormous. Some had been former VIs who were drafted into the RSS and into uniform. A few lived locally and went home after shift. Others who came from elsewhere lived on camp and they were a very fine bunch of men for whom I had the greatest respect. They were mainly middle aged, some even older, and they came from widely different backgrounds. This was reflected in the way they spent their off duty periods. Many had hobbies and leather-work was one that was very popular. One a Scot, was a violinist who would often stand outside the hut and play to his heart's content. Another was a learned chap who could well have been a school teacher and when he found that I was interested in butterflies and moths, would talk to me about Darwin's theory of evolution and similar subjects. In the main I never found out much about the background of these gentlemen but they were excellent fellows to share a hut with. It was particularly noticeable that they were all of sober habits and I cannot recall any of them going out to pubs when off duty. Though those that went home every day after shift we got to know some local people which resulted in some very pleasant social relationships. I would describe these worthy gentlemen as civilians who had been put in uniform for either convenience or for administration purposes. They were not soldiers in the full sense of the word. Already demobilisation had been planned by the government and men were to be released in a numbered sequence, based on length of service and age. Ex-prisoners of war were given an almost immediate discharge. Under a special regulation RSS men were to be released based on 'The Services for Which They Enlisted Being No Longer Required.'

However there was one old man who looked every inch a soldier. He lived nearby and worked day duty only. He used to arrive each morning and his firsts act was to get a cup of tea. He must have been 70 years old and wore his uniform well. He never wore the standard issue beret but instead wore a peaked cap, after the style of the Guards with the peak almost touching his nose. He had rows of ribbons on his tunic indicating that he had served in WWI and other conflicts prior to that. He often told me stories of his service which included his part in a firing squad in the execution of a spy in WWI. He must have had a signals telegraphist background because he could send and receive Morse on the land line. Other than that he seemed to do odd jobs around the station. He was quiet an unforgettable character.[1]

Our cook was also another unforgettable character. He was a Scot who was naturally called Jock. I do not know what his background was but he was in uniform and I think he may also have lived locally. He got along well with everyone, providing there were not disparaging remarks made about Robbie Burns. As a cook he served us well. There seemed to be no shortage of anything and when coming off night duty Jock would have our breakfast ready, plates full of fried eggs, bacon and porridge prepared the Scottish way and toast. Having come from England where everything was strictly rationed this was like living in another world. The other meals served up by Jock were of an equally high standard. His contribution to the war effort could not be underrated.

The third category of men at the station, possibly around ten in number was remarkable different from the others. They were men in their late 20s and early 30s who had seen service overseas, most likely in army units involved in signals and some intercept work. It is known that the army, navy and air force each had their own intercept branches. These men were already in place when I arrived so I have no idea when they arrived or where they came from.

1 I believe the gentleman Ray is referring to was a Mr Wiley who served during WWI with the Royal Engineers Signals regiment. I spoke to his son and he recalled his father's connections to the GPO and Gilnahirk during WWII. His son also remembered Captain Banham coming to the family home at Knockvale Park and collecting his father on a number of occasions.

They had campaign ribbons on their tunics which from memory indicated the North African and Italian campaigns. Some were lance corporals and some were corporals and I suspect that they brought these stripes with them. These stripes may have been hard won in the ranks from wherever they came from and they were very conscious of them, which was in marked contrast to the RSS men who had stripes because they were supervisors and had little or nothing to do with discipline. Some of these men were quite arrogant and hard drinkers. It is not known how they were paid, whether it was their ordinary army rates or whether they had a top up to RSS rates. We still received our pay in envelopes each week and it was almost a private arrangement, we did not talk about it. Generally, this disparate collection of men worked well together and I do not want to infer that there were any personal problems between them. They were just different.

Social life at Gilnahirk was very pleasant, Belfast was close and a favourite place to eat when in town was a restaurant called 'Campbells'. There was also a place in a poorer residential area where we took our washing. The lady was glad of the business and one could have all your clothes washed and ironed for a few shillings.

Social life for young men inevitably involved young women and there were dances and other social events. However, one has to admit that there were some problems stemming from religious affiliations. Lasting relationships were difficult if one party was Roman Catholic and the other Protestant. This did not bother me unduly as my mother was Catholic (of Irish Connection) and my father was Protestant and they had married in an English setting where the difference was not noticeable. So I felt that I had a foot in each camp and quite comfortable in any relationship.

Although visitors to the camp at Crofton Hall were generally discouraged, we were allowed to have guests in the canteen on Sunday evenings. These led to some very jolly times and friends tended to bring friends and the attitude would be that there were no strangers, only friends that you had not yet met, so there was always someone to say "they are with me." This led to much singing of Irish songs and Irish dancing and of course drinking, but everyone was on their best behaviour. The only drink available was Guinness, which everyone seems to like. I should add that our canteen was one of the few places in Belfast where one could get a drink on a Sunday.

The early summer of 1945 was wonderful for several reasons. The weather was good and there were some lovely places to visit during days off duty. I do not require the words of the old song to tell me how many miles it is from Bangor to Donaghadee because I have had the great pleasure of walking the distance. It was also the time of the unconditional surrender of Germany, and I was given home leave which was by the overnight ferry from Belfast to Heysham, itself an experience not to be missed by a young fellow. Before leaving there was shopping to be done. The shops were full of things made from Irish linen embroidered with clovers and I bought quite a selection. There was also another ritual for anyone going on leave to England that was paying a visit to a farm located quite close to the station at Gilnahirk. It was a short walk the day before your last shift to advise the farmer or his wife that you were going on leave. Then on your last day you called at the farm and collected the items they had set aside for you, mainly fresh eggs. The whole thing cost just a few shillings but with eggs being rationed in England to one per person per week a box of eggs from the farm at Gilnahirk was most welcome.

On return from leave I settled into the camp life again, this time it was post war, at least as far as the interceptors were concerned and the talk was of demobilisation. My 'demob' number was 65 so I knew that civilian life was not imminent for me, but it was for many of the older RSS men who had wives, houses and mostly jobs in civilian life to return to. In August we heard about the atomic bomb being dropped on to Japanese cities and the final surrender. Everyone then began to think about the future, for themselves, the station and the service. The General Election that followed saw Attlee take over from Churchill as Prime Minister.

By this time I was approaching my 19th birthday and having reached that milestone in life the opportunity to volunteer for overseas service. To my surprise I was immediately accepted and in October said my farewells to Knock and Gilnahirk and returned to Arkley for further training and an array of vaccinations followed by embarkation leave. There were about a dozen young fellows in the draft, most had been serving in other RSS stations. Our destination was in the middle east but we were told to say nothing about our destination, not even to family members. Our location was screened by an address comprising a series of abbreviations. It was deemed to be "on active service" and we all speculated on what that might be.

This ends my recollections of Gilnahirk, they are pleasant memories but now many years after the event I can only wish that I had written all this down much sooner. If I had it probably would have been more interesting and much more informative."

Another document which I came across in my research was the diary of one Lieutenant Leslie Luscombe, a Royal signals officer based at Barnet who, towards the end of the war, was tasked with taking a shipment of new equipment to Gilnahirk where he was to oversee its installation. The following account from his wartime diary refers to the installation of additional receivers and equipment at Station No 4 and gives a fascinating insight into the frustrations even high priority work had to face with a military organisation.

INSTALLATION OF RECEIVERS AND EQUIPMENT AT NO 4 STATION

30.08.44   Acting on instructions from Lt Col Cole Adams, I visited the L.M.S. Offices at Watford to make the necessary arrangements to transport the equipment and myself to Belfast via Heysham.I arrived at Watford at 1215 and met by Yabsley, Transport Managers Dept. Hut A5, Tel: Watford 6464, ext. 228. Mr Yabsley said that this matter should be settled through the Movement Control Authorities. I mentioned that the position was rather different inasmuch the apparatus was most fragile and secret and that it was essential that I accompanied it throughout the journey. Accommodation was eventually found for myself and the stores on the Mail Boat leaving Heysham at 2355 on 02.09.44, arriving Belfast at 0630, 03.09.44. Normally goods are not carried by mail boat and we have Mr Yabsley to thank for permitting this. Mention was made that the Military authorities permit only high ranking officers to travel on the Heysham route and that I would have to obtain a movement order covering this. I returned to Signals Group and Major Bellringer advised Lt Col Cole Adams regarding this point, at the same time arranging accommodation at Hanslope for Thursday evening, 31st August, and through Lancs, Constabulary arranged accommodation at Heysham for the nights of Friday, 1st September and Saturday, 2nd September, for the lorry driver and myself.

31.8.44 19:00hrs Arrived Hanslope by Duty Car – contacted Engineering Section and also enquired if form G980 has been completed. This has not been done. Lt Col Cole Adams took my blank forms and completed them.

1.9.44 08:00hrs Left Hanslope with S.C.U.1 truck No 4159426, driver Signalman McCurry, Equipment was packed in thirteen crates weighing approximately 11 cwt.

09:45hrs Arrived Atherstone.

12:00hrs Arrived Stone.

12:15hrs Hixon. Filled up with petrol at RAF aerodrome.

17:05hrs Lancaster

17:10hrs Decided to contact dock authorities tonight instead of tomorrow in case of difficulties.

18:00hrs Arrived Heysham docks and went to E.S.O. office. Capt Fry (E.S.O.) not there until morning but NCO, after inspecting my papers, said that I would not be able to travel as the Heysham route was only for privilege or compassionate leave travel. (There is an A.C.I. to this effect). Major Sclater through Major Bellringer had arranged to notify Movement Control and Security Officers, Heysham, of my proposed visit but E.S.O. office new nothing of this. I therefore asked E.S.O. TO check through security section. This was done. E.S.O. were told that they (Security) would pass me through OK but could not give authority for travel by Heysham route. I then made appointment to see Captain Fry (E.S.O.) at 09:00hrs on Saturday morning, 2.9.44.

21:30hrs Phoned Hanslope – made contact with Miss Charlton and told her that I expected difficulties and suggested that someone phoned the E.S.O.'s office and quoted some authority for the journey to Heysham, also if I failed to get aboard with the equipment, should I send it across and advise Major Banham accordingly. Miss Charlton said that she would endeavour to get advice on these matters and I promised to phone next morning.

1.9.44 22:00hrs Proceeded to Lancaster Police H.Q. and met Superintendent who had arranged hotel and Y.M.C.A. accommodation for myself and driver and garage in the police yard for our truck. The police transported the driver and myself by police car on our several journeys to and from hotel and Police H.Q. Police extremely helpful during our visit and I suggest that a note of thanks should be sent through Capt. Stanworth or ourselves.
2.9.44 08:45hrs Reported to E.S.O. Heysham docks (Capt. Fry) who was most annoyed about the whole affair saying that apart from the fact that I had no authority to travel, the whole arrangement, i/e cabin accommodation, transportation of crates, garage and accommodation for driver myself, should have been arranged through E.S.O. Capt. Fry showed me the A.C.I. relating to travel for services from Heysham and said that it was more than he dare to grant permission. I told him the job was urgent and operational and the apparatus secret, explaining that if I were prevented from travelling, the apparatus would not be able to leave either and suggested that if I had to return to H.Q. with the equipment, someone would most certainly be sorry about it. I stated also that the equipment was to be operational early Monday and that I would be working on the installation of same on Sunday and throughout the night. I did this in an endeavour to stress the urgency and importance. This appeared to have the desired effect and the E.S.O. eventually agreed to let me sail, with repeated threats of making complaints about me to the war office.

09:45hrs Phone Miss Charlton at H.Q. and reported that difficulties were now overcome and suggested that Major Sclater or someone phone E.S.O. to quieten him down a little, stressing the fact that this had better be done after I had sailed in case of any misunderstanding that might arise again.

10:30hrs Filled lorry with petrol at Heysham Towers.

18:30hrs Proceeded to docks with lorry and met L.M.S. Officials. Personally supervised loading of cases, thirteen in all, on to Mail Boat and say them locked up in G.P.O. Mail Cabin.

21:30hrs Went through E.S.O. officially and received embarkation ticket.

21:45hrs Went through security section. Saw numerous service people re-directed to Stanraer route and considered myself fortunate.

22:00hrs Thanked Capt. Fry, who had calmed down and embarked at 22:30hrs. (Capt. Fry said that he would let it pass this time but he did not want things like this to happen every day. Personally I do not think that the matter will go any further now.)

3.9.44 01:00hrs Sailed from Heysham

09:30hrs Arrived Belfast. More difficulties as everyone else had a travel warrant – I had not. Officials said that I could not possibly have come aboard without one, which made a suitable answer difficult. Fortunately, Lt Bright was on the dockside and knew the officials concerned and I managed to get off the boat again, personally supervising the unloading of the crates.

10:30hrs Loaded gear on to lorry and proceeded to No 4 Station. Proceeded to unpack crates and get to work on the installation of receivers. This work was finally completed on Monday 11th September, and I returned by air to Barnet arriving 16:30, where I reported to Signals Group.

The installation of six double bank receivers and equipment with "split phones" and "isolated working" switches. "Compare signal" facilities were also provided between banks and a circuit was provided between banks and concentrator with two way calling and speaking for putting signals to line. A panel was constructed containing necessary switching, lamps and microphones. Two 30ft poles were erected from which six aerials fed receivers – 2 inverted L's and 4 long wire types.

Considerable difficulty was experienced in getting the power supply connected by the local authority, a fault having developed on the cable outside. Much pressure was used by Major Banham both before my arrival and after to get the job expedited, but nevertheless it was Sunday, 9th September, before power was restored. The cable is too small for the load it has to carry and the voltage drop is very severe at times, sufficient to impair the working of the receivers. Tests made show 200 volts at one period and 185 at another. Major Banham is getting this matter rectified as soon as possible. Having no power impeded progress considerably through soldering and lighting difficulties.

The size of the poles (weight) necessitated digging two 5ft holes and this job was impossible until Friday owing to heavy rain which was continuous from the time I arrived until the Friday. As the station was to be in operation on Saturday mid-day the delay in obtaining the electrical supply and having to erect the aerials caused some fast and hard work to be done by men assisting me.

Further complications were caused by:

1. Non-locking type switches were sent and replacements had to be sent by air.
2. Out of the 14 pairs of CHR headsets, 4 sets were dis.
3. The 100 yards of flex ordered was not sent.
4. Of the 12 power packs despatched, 2 were 110 volts (one of which was faulty) and in another the rectifier valve was not functioning. When I attempted to replace the rectifier, I discovered that the 86 valve holder had been replaced by a British 4-pin holder and British rectifier, a type of which no replacement was available. The pins at the base of the valve had already been re-soldered and a dry joint was found on one of the heater pins.
5. On 7m – 14 coil faulty. One Broadcast .9 – 2.05 coil completely broken – condenser and coil frame lying in pieces inside can.
6. One H.R.O. condenser drive faulty, slipping on shaft.
7. The metal panels for fastening the sets and power packs together and carrying the key switch were made, to my measurements, and would have been quite satisfactory if the usual type of power pack had been used. Instead of this, apart from two, all the power packs were the old type of narrow section and this involved cutting and re-drilling all the panels to suit the old power packs.

The main concentrator panel in the station into which I had to couple our makeshift unit from the extension station appears to be in need of an overhaul. Apparently various people have worked on this board making alterations and fault finding etc. and the wiring is in a very bad way. Leads have been disconnected all over the place and left hanging with bare ends. Some wires are bared in places and all sorts of intermittent troubles occur. The engineer attached to No 4 Station, considering the isolated position of the station, is not too well provided with tools and miscellaneous stores, (i.e.) screws, flex, solder, etc., etc. The engineer in question was most helpful and gave every assistance possible.

Major Banham would like the 2 power packs, flex and 4 sets of head-phones replaced as soon as possible, on receipt of which he will return the unsuitable and faulty equipment together with the 6 non-locking type switches.

(Signed) L. Luscombe

Lieut., Royal Signals

S.C.U.3 14TH September 1944 lhl/awl

Given that by the time Leiut. Luscome was working at Gilnahirk the Allies have already liberated Paris and the Normandy landings continue to push the Nazis forces back towards Germany. Perhaps this installation of new equipment was undertaken due to the momentum built up during the war but one can't help speculating as to whether it was to support the existing conflict or was someone already looking at the role of Post War interception at Gilnahirk?

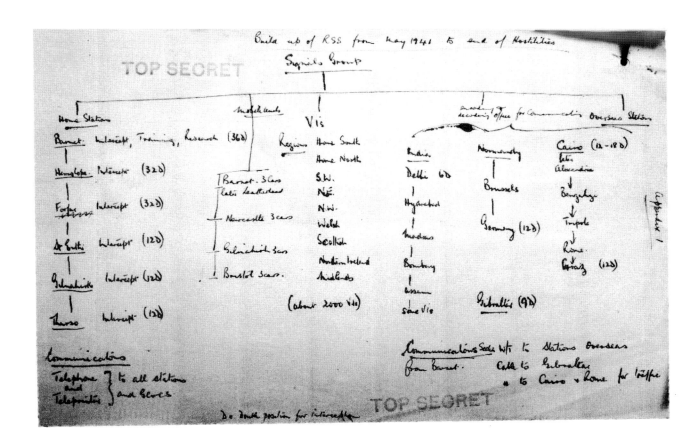

At the cessation of hostilities in 1945 the RSS had grown to be a substantial organisation as shown in the hand written organisation chart above. However like all branches of the military it was subject to major upheaval in the wake of the conflict.

Gilnahirk was not excluded from this upheval and a perusal of the logs of Alan Sharpe who was posted there on 11th Nov 1944 give a little insight into what was happening.

Alan's letter of enlistment

Alan Sharpe had an above average knowledge and understanding of wireless and prior to his call up had been working with picture wire machines for the Daily Sketch newspaper which were used to send pictures electronically from one location to another.

Perhaps as a result of his technical ability Alan had come to the attention of the Radio Security Service as just the sort of person they were looking for and he was interviewed on 18 March 1944 by Major Bellringer of the Radio Security Service with a view to enlistment although naturally Alan would have to be positively vetted before his recruitment would go any further.

Having successfully secured a clean bill of health from the vetting process Major Bellringer offered Alan an enlistment within the RSS and instructed him to report for duty at 'Arkley View', Arkley, Barnet on Saturday morning 22 April 1944. This was the Headquarter of the RSS, the mysterious PO Box 25.

On 24 April 1944 Alan Sharpe took the Oath of Allegiance and signed on the dotted line to become a serving member of the Royal Signals Corps. However, although he wore a military uniform he was not in the army and he was not paid by the army and in his pay book it states *"This soldier has been enlisted for special duty. Whilst on that special duty this man is entitled to wear civilian clothes."* The Royal Signals uniform was simply a cover and his service number, which began with the figures two six zero (2603045) hid a secret. Alan was now working for British Military Intelligence.

Having successfully completed his induction and training courses into the RSS Alan was posted to Hanslope Park where he spent some months. The work at Hanslope involved the inspection and realignment of HRO receives which were coming in from the United States under the lend lease agreement and Alan's duty was to bring these American HRO receivers up to the highest specifications possible for use in the work of radio interception.

HRO receiver with interchangeable coils for various frequency ranges

After some months at Hanslope Alan received a movement order which would take him to Belfast, Northern Ireland on the 11 November 1944.

Robin Sharpe had retained his father's logs from the war and kindly let me see those covering the period from 17 November 1944 up to and including 6 July 1945 which gave details of the work carried out by his father at the Station No 4 site. Alan's duty was to calibrate, service, and repair the radio equipment as well as carrying out any general maintenance which may have been required to keep the station operational.

In the log entry for 22 December 1944 Major Banham is mentioned – evidently Captain Banham had been promoted since he had come to Northern Ireland. Although I do not have a date for this, I suspect it happened around the time that Gilnahirk became a fully military operation.

Alan's logs also reveal the names of some of both the other military and civilian personnel who were serving at Station No 4 during this period including:

Major Keen, Major Poole. Captain Beadon, Captain Bennett. Company Sergeant Major George. Sergeant Major McLoughlin, Sergeant Graham, Sergeant Hepworth, Sergeant Holdsworth, Sergeant Matlock, Sergeatn Price. Lance Corporal Thomas. Signalman Bladon,

Signalman Caufort, Signalman Galpin, Signalman Wilson. We then have two surnames but no rank, French and Middleton. Then civilians Mr. Bright, Mr Browning (DCRE), Mr. Finney and finally the surname Noakes who phones from Barnet.

During his time at Station No 4 Alan experienced some tension between a Captain Beadon and the non-commissioned ranks over the shortage of serviceable equipment at Gilnahirk but this shortage of operational equipment was relieved somewhat when a shipment of fourteen receivers arrived from Hanslope Park on the 25 March 1945.

Interestingly Alan's logs also reveal that there were radio receivers at Crofton Hall which seems rather unusual and right at the end of WWII in Europe an entry dated 6 May 1945 reveals that a total of fifty-two radio receivers were accounted for at Station No 4 by Alan.

The following day 7 May 1945 Alan is on leave making the most of the Victory in Europe celebrations across the nation and just over two weeks later as a consequence of this victory he makes two significant entries in his log

25 May 1945. "Take complete stock of contents of General Search station and submit to Sgt Irwin. General Search will finish at midnight."

26 May 1945. "Off Duty. Mobile takes over General Search Hut."

These entries officially declare the termination of the General Search operation after five long years of service.

Alan's final entry was dated 6 July 1945 and states:

Remove fan from roof, clean and reassemble parts taken down. Fit 100/250 to ? knight frequency. Standard for D/F. Check auxiliary power supply plant with Lance Corporal Thomas. Advised at 4pm of my new posting back to Hanslope Park.

Alan was discharged from his enlistment on 5th October 1946

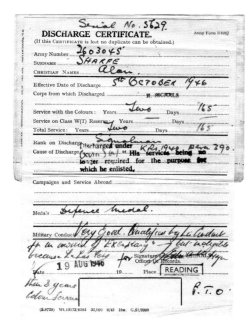

Discharge papers

As the new world order became established in the aftermath of the carnage of WWII the war it was clearer than ever that signals intelligence was a vital component in the defence of the realm. Knowledge is power and understanding what both your friends and your foes are doing would prove vital during the post war years as erstwhile allies realigned and relationships cooled as the cold war got underway.

Although war time agreements between British and American Intelligence meant that the Americans were fully aware of Bletchley Park's successes, the Soviet Union had never been officially told what went on there. Although in later years it emerged that the Russians had an agent, John Cairncross, in Bletchley Park who had been passing them the highest grade intelligence material, most of the world was unaware of the achievements of the Allies signals intelligence operations and the government felt it best that it remain that way.

Thus Bletchly Park was shut down and, discretely, the Government Code and Cypher School (the code breakers from Bletchley Park) was rebranded as Government Communications Headquarters (GCHQ) in June 1946. The new organisation would bring the various signals intelligence groups together and thus the RSS was incorporated into GCHQ. Initially based in Eastcote before moving to Cheltenham in 1951, if anything, GCHQ sought to adopt an even lower profile than Bletchley Park and the veil of secrecy was pulled down ever tighter.

It seems from Alan Sharpe's account that the main WWII function of the Gilnahirk wireless station site, the general search ceased in May 1945, presumably as a side effect of the overall reorganisation of the signals intelligence operations. While the GPO records granted me an insight into the debates and thinking that was going on when Gilnahirk was facing closure in 1942 I do not have any similar information into what happened in the aftermath of WWII.

Some I have spoken to have indicated that aspects of the station remained operational. In Alan Sharpe's logs he records that the mobile unit remained in place despite the closure of the General Search and many of the VIs still remained active as confirmed by these character references given to Dr Joe Parke who still seems to have been working for GCHQ as late as 1956.

Another indicator that any break in operations at Gilnahirk was at most a temporary measure is the amount of equipment being shipped in towards the end of the war according to both Luscome and Sharpe. If the base was about to close, why bring all this equipment in?

Whatever the reasoning and planning, in July 1947 the wireless receivers at Gilnahirk were switched on again and the station was back in business. Everything would continue as before, but the primary target in this war was the threat of Communism. As the Iron Curtain closed across Europe the world had entered

This from an interview with Edna Cobain nee Lamour who lived on the wireless station's doorstep.
"My father bought the McDowell farm in 1946 after the death of brother and sister Ellen and Frank McDowell. It was a small holding of only a few acres. (Edna's memories of the station were clear, despite the passing of time.) Having reopened in 1947 for operation these are my primary memories of the wireless station. Within the field in front of our house was a brick building. This was a large square building and could be entered by a porch. Once inside Edna could see a number of both men and women working away. In one room on the right there were a great number of teleprinters and long lengths of teleprinter tape coming off these machines."

I should add that Edna was only a child when she was befriended by many of the female staff who came to her father's farm for eggs. With the farm being on the doorstep of the station it became her playground and on many occasions she accompanied the female staff members as they moved from location to location around the site.

"In the field opposite the farm was a large wooden building, black in color. This was the wartime GPO station. It appeared that only ladies worked within the building and it was entered by a small porch at the side. Edna was never allowed to enter this building but sometimes the ladies would open the windows and speak out to her as she played in the field. Her father was allowed to take the hay off the field. On a good summers day, the ladies would lie out on the grass and enjoy a bit of sun bathing. Access to this building was gained by walking along a small path and through a gate from the Lisleen Road East. On one occasion two ladies from this cont over...

the Cold War, a period of tension that would last for almost fifty years.

Although Gilnahirk was up and running again there had been several changes from the war time operation including the introduction of female staff. The radio equipment in long wooden bungalow building must have been stripped out as this was now the home of the clerical side of the work. The listening operation was conducted entirely from within the brick buildings located in the WWII camp field in front of McDowell's farm. The late John Haslett a radio operator at the site recalls walking from where he worked in the brick buildings over to the wooden bungalow with files or paperwork for the ladies.

Many of the male staff are ex-service, some are ex merchant marine and for a few this is their second posting to Gilnahirk. Mr. Norman Graham ex Royal Signals (his cover whilst working for MI8c) had served with the Radio Security Service, SCU 3 during WWII, but I believe there were also others. I was also informed that a great many of those men who were engaged in this postwar work across the British Isles had been specially recruited because of their previous experience and association with the wartime work of both the Special Communications and Special Liaison Units. These were the units responsible for the interception and handling of the Ultra material generated by Bletchley Park.

While the work of the D/F station may possibly have continued uninterrupted after 1945 (although it was part of the site, it could function as a standalone facility under Barnet Control) towards the end of 1948, beginning of 1949 the Underground Cabin was abandoned. Robin Morrow on whose land the cabin was located told me it had been filled in and was never recovered from its buried location. Crockery ducting and cables feeding the Cabin have been unearthed but the metal tank remains in place to this day.

This high frequency direction finding facility was moved some seven miles across country to Island Hill on the shores of Strangford Lough outside Comber. Working above ground everything was contained within a wooden hut placed just above the ground, but sitting on a mat of coiled copper wire. Apart from these few facts I know nothing more about the workings of this facility.

For the officer in charge at Gilnahirk Wireless Station it was a welcome return to the establishment he had commanded from its first day of world war two operations in 1940 until the final day of operations in 1945. Major Joe Banham was back. This time in civilian clothes, but still working for the same wartime organization that had rebranded itself the Government Communications Headquarters, (GCHQ). In reality very little had changed and the postwar operation would continue to follow the experience gained during WWII. It was still the same secret location that no one talked about, least of all those who worked there. It was a place where questions were never asked because answers would not be forth coming.

Although security was very tight at Gilnahirk with staff strictly forbidden to speak about what they were doing this did not mean they lived in a complete bubble. On any forms they had to complete they would record their occupations as Government Service, a front they would maintain in their lives outside work. As the late Mr George McCullough of Elsmere Park explained to his wife when he took up employment at Gilnahirk

> "From this day forward you are not to speak of my work
> to anyone including our family. If asked any questions you
> will say that I am an Imperial civil servant working for
> Stormont, and that is all you and they need to know."

On a lighter note, due to this Civil Service connection the station had a football team that played in the Northern Ireland Civil Service League Championship. Known simply as the Gilnahirk GCRS

cont...

wooden building called at the farm for eggs. They were also taking lunch to the gentleman at the D/F location. I was allowed to go with them. The D/F tank (the underground cabin) was located on the crest of the hill just a short distance from the farm. Four very large wooden poles marked the location and it was towards these that they were walking. On reaching the center of the poles the two ladies bent over and took hold of two metal rings. They then began to pull these rings upwards and to Edna's amazement a hole in the grass field appeared from nowhere. It was like something out of a CS Lewis story. This was the access hatch to a buried metal tank. Climbing down a steep metal ladder she met and spoke with a gentleman who was wearing headphones and sitting in front of some radio equipment. It was all most interesting to me. During the life of the reopened station the ministry had tried unsuccessfully to obtain water by sinking a number of wells, three in total. A small river which ran along the bottom of my father's field had become a source of water for the farm. With the agreement of her father the ministry was allowed to create a twenty-six feet deep well at this location which then filled from the river. A small brick pump house was constructed to bring the water up to the station complex. I also recall regular visits to the farm for eggs by Major Joe Banham and I also remember the daily ritual of burning the waste in a small brick hut with a chimney on the top. A fire lighter was used to make the whole process very quick and effective. It roared like a rocket and created a great deal of flame which shot out of the chimney." The brick pump house remains on site to this day and the well is capped with a large concrete cover.

Football Club. It consisted of the following members of staff. A.J. Allen. (Capt.) G. Giff. T. Drake. J.F. Milburn. D. Lewis. S. Bunting. H. Cambridge. R. Field. R.M. Wallace. W.R. Holmes. F. McMechan. Supporting the players, E. Cairnduff (Trainer) and five others in various roles. N.F. Dearden. S. Vogan. P. Campblisson. N.A. Morton. W. Grayson. J.H. Roden. The 1950 season finished with the team from Gilnahirk winning the cup.

(Gilnahirk GCRS = Government Communications Radio Station).

However developments at Gilnahirk were far from over and within three years of switch on, the powers that be in GCHQ decided to upgrade the wartime facility by building a completely new wireless station.

This involved the transfer of the listening / interception operation into temporary wooden huts erected parallel with the Gilnahirk road which allowed the existing brick buildings to be completely removed to make way for the new station building. Security was extremely tight during the new construction phase and it fell to a detachment of Military Police officers of the Vunerable Points branch who remained on site twenty-four seven. Created during the early years of WWII the VP Section were assigned the protection of high value military and government assets, plus the protection of key individuals in society. Eventually the new building was ready and everyone, both male and female came together under one roof. Officially known as Composite Signals Organisation Station Gilnahirk this was just one of a series of GCHQ listening stations both at home and abroad. Despite this amalgamation of the sexes there were strict lines of demarcation drawn within the building which was made up of four elements. The main block was a two storey structure which contained various offices on the ground floor. These were occupied by both male and female staff members. Upstairs I am informed was the location of Traffic Analysis which was manned by the female staff. Downstairs to the rear of the main block was the 'Set Room' the heart of the listening / interception operation. This was a male dominated area where the various watches conducted their duty.

Added to both sides of the main block were two extensions running parallel with the set room. On the left the male locker room, a kitchen, male toilets, plus a stores and wireless workshop for repairs. On the right a similar configuration for the female staff, but also a strong room, the telephone equipment rooms and the 'Typex' room. Keeping the sexes firmly apart was strictly controlled and all female staff

The station in 1951. Some of the many aerials which surrounded the facility and marched across the castlereagh Hills can just be picked out as can the edge of the Wullenweber array (lower right)

were expected to dress in accordance to civil service rules. No slacks or trousers, skirts and dresses only. Failure to comply and you were sent home. Improper relationships between the sexes was strictly forbidden and no two members of staff with a family connection were allowed to work at the same location. By 1953 the new station was up and running. Officially the site was known as Composite Signals Organisation Station Gilnahirk. Almost one hundred personnel, both male and female manned the station on a 24/7 three hundred and sixty-five days a year basis. Surrounding the new station, were twenty-nine 100Fft steel towers arranged in various ways to capture any signal from the ether.

Sometime later (at a date and time I have been unable to establish) Gilnahirk was equipped with a German system of high frequency direction finding known as the Wullenweber. This consisted of two rings of aerials with an operator's hut placed in the centre of the smaller circle.

Of course N. Ireland people are well known for their inquisitiveness and the appearance of a notice to tender for the construction a new radio station at Gilnahirk did not go un-noticed but although questions may have been asked no answers were given as this article from the *Belfast Telegraph* in August 1951 illustrates:

New Radio Station sets Northern Ireland Riddle.
Nobody knows at Gilnahirk.
A new radio station is to be erected at Gilnahirk, near Belfast. Today the Ministry of Finance invited tenders for the erection and completion of the station, but behind the Ministry's announcement lies a mystery. Who is the station for and for what purpose is it going to be used? The Ministry of Finance know nothing about it. They have only been asked to get the station built and there an official says, as far as the Ministry is concerned, the matter ends. Is it for the BBC? Apparently not. At Broadcasting House in Belfast the BBC say nothing to do with us. Do the police intend to use the station? The answer is again "No." The Royal Air Force say it's "not for us."
Already there is a radio station but the address is not given in the telephone directory. A call to "Directory Inquiries" brings the reply: "The number has been withheld at the request of the subscriber. I am sorry we cannot help you more"
But the site can be contacted by telephoning the RAF Station at Dundonald. The operator there will put a caller through to Gilnahirk and no questions are asked. It is different when Gilnahirk replies. "Who is calling," the telephonist wants to know, "and why." She cannot answer questions. Apart from her job of answering the telephone she does not know what goes on there, she says. Her superiors confess to not knowing either. A pleasant voiced Englishman says, "I am sorry, old man, I do not really know what happens." And then talking to him is like trying to get an answer from a wall. "What do you do there?" He

---

New radio station sets N.I. riddle
Nobody knows—at Gilnahirk
"Belfast Telegraph" Reporter.

A NEW radio station is to be erected at Gilnahirk, near Belfast. To-day the Ministry of Finance invited tenders for the erection and completion of the station, but behind the Ministry's announcement lies a mystery. "Who is the station for and for what purpose is it going to be used?"

The Ministry of Finance know nothing about it. They have only been asked to get the station built, and there an official says, as far as the Ministry is concerned, the matter ends.

Is it for the B.B.C.? Apparently not. At Broadcasting House in Belfast the B.B.C. say "Nothing to do with us."

Do the police intend to use the station? The answer is again "No."

The Royal Air Force say it is "not for us."

Already at Gilnahirk there is a radio station but the address is not given in the telephone directory.

A call to "Directory Inquiries" brings the reply: "The number has been withheld at the request of the subscriber. I am sorry we cannot help you more."

But the site can be contacted by telephoning the R.A.F. station at Dundonald. The operator there will put a caller through to Gilnahirk and no questions are asked.

It is different when Gilnahirk replies. "Who is calling," the telephonist wants to know, "and why."

She cannot answer

She cannot answer questions. Apart from her job of answering the telephone she does not know what goes on there, she says.

Her superiors confess to not knowing either. A pleasant voiced Englishman says, "I am sorry, old man, I do not really know what happens."

And then talking to him is like trying to get an answer from a wall. "What do you do there?" He does not know.

"What is the existing station used for?" He does not know.

"Why is a second station being built?" He does not know.

"Has it anything to do with the Royal Air Force?" He does know —it has nothing to do with the flying service.

does not know. "What is the existing station used for?" He does not know. "Has it anything to do with the Royal Air Force?" He does know, it has nothing to do with the flying service.

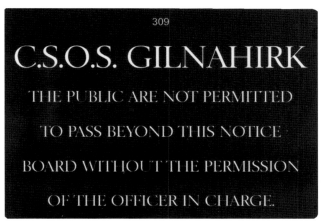

309

C.S.O.S. GILNAHIRK

THE PUBLIC ARE NOT PERMITTED

TO PASS BEYOND THIS NOTICE

BOARD WITHOUT THE PERMISSION

OF THE OFFICER IN CHARGE.

A sign at the gate of Gilnahirk which meant what it said

Although it was undoubtedly extremely frustrating for the reporter who from the tone of his article, undoubtedly felt he was facing a conspiracy of deceit from everyone he talked to might have been surprised to know how many were actually telling the truth – they really didn't know.

When my research began I approached a number of those retired Cold War employees who still resided in the Gilnahirk area for any knowledge of anything that may have been said about events during WWII. In all cases the answer was the same over and over again, *"I am sorry Mr Busby, but I have signed the official secrets act and I can say nothing."*

Disappointing as it may be I had to respect what had been said and leave it at that.

As the years progressed and my research began to reveal the history and purpose of WWII some of the former employees began to talk. Not about secrets but about the security and I began to see how most if not all the people mentioned in the Belfast Telegraph article may have been telling the truth.

As one former radio operator explained.

> "The thing to remember is that within GCHQ things are very compartmented. You were not allowed to ask the people in the next office what they did. The pass you wore around your neck not only gave your security clearance, it proclaimed which offices or areas you were allowed access to. Working for the Composite Signals Organisation was akin to those Russian "Matryoshka" dolls where you open

one doll to find another identical inside, open it and there's another inside it. Right down to the very tiny one in the centre. If a colleague vanished for a few months, you were not encouraged to ask where he had been. People were often gliding off on short tours to semi-open stations – such as Turkey and Iran. They were accepted as short tours and could be – after a fashion – discussed. However, interspersed amongst these were what were called the 'suitcase' jobs. these special operations were VRK (Very Restricted Knowledge) the highest security level and all had their own 'code word' – the code word itself being top secret – you can see how difficult it would be to ascertain exactly what anyone within the organisation was up to."

Clerical staff knew even less about what was going on as one female staff member explained as she recalled her time at Gilnahirk.

"I worked in the Northern Ireland Civil Service and on the occasion of my marriage I had to leave the service because married women were not employed. I heard through the grapevine that a typist was being recruited by the Imperial Civil Service at a location in Northern Ireland close to my home. When I applied for the post I was interviewed by a Mr D Harrison who unknown to me at the time was the officer in charge at CSOS Gilnahirk. I was told that the vetting process would take about three months and if successful I would be employed. I began work in 1966 and remained at the station until the birth of my daughter in 1969. A typical day for myself was nine to five and my primary duty was a typist to the Officer in Charge plus clerical duties. I did not receive any special training for the job. I worked Monday to Friday and I was never called upon to do anything different. I never had to stand in for anyone other than the clerk in my office. It was his task to man the telephone switch board. There were two other gentlemen in the same office, HCO Mr Eric Smith and CA Mr Jim Downey. In an adjoining office was another HCO Mr Stanley Hall. Under my terms of employment, I was not given the free run of the station, just where I had to go, the OIC's office, the Station Operations Office and the Radio Repair Shop. At no time during my employment did anything of a secret nature pass across my desk or come before my eyes. I was allowed unto the first floor at lunchtime where I played table tennis with some of the other ladies and had my lunch in the lady's recreational area. Other rooms on this second floor were strictly off limits to me. I was one very small cog in a big machine and I knew absolutely nothing or never asked questions about the work of the station."

Another insight into the levels of security was given by Brian Woodward, an apprentice electrician with the Ministry of Public Buildings and Works based at the Royal Naval Air Yard at Sydenham. The MPBW were responsible for the general day to day maintenance of many government buildings and establishments including Gilnahirk and Brian recalled his visits to the wireless station.

"When a job came up for Gilnahirk Wireless Station everyone tried to get off side, it was not the place anyone wished to work at. Once the works transport had dropped you off at the wireless station gate you were there until the transport came back to collect you at the end of the working day. You could complete your job in less than an hour, but be confined within the station for five or six hours at a stretch.

On arrival at the main gate security took you straight to the gentlemen's locker room within the main building. Stone floored with small windows high up this was like a prison cell. There you would sit on long wooden benches until the room / office or work space you were going to work in was prepared. Large white sheets would cover everything, tables, filling cabinets even stuff on the walls. Once each job was completed in one location you were taken back to the locker room where you had to wait for the concealment of the next work space. On and on it went, complete madness to say the least. The main set room, the heart of the listening operation could not be completely concealed, but before entering you were told not to look about you, not to ask questions and to be in and out as quickly as possible. Within the main set room, I recall large reel to reel tape recorders at each of the operator's work stations. Men with headphones were continually listening and writing, some were using typewriters to record what they heard. Other men were working at desks, checking book indexes of some kind. I recall one man being told to encrypt something and send it off at once. One man who I assumed was in charge was standing on a platform overlooking the whole room and behind him looked like what I shall call a large plug board. It was a very strange set up and it was nice to complete your work and get out of there.

Just off this main room was a section manned by ladies and off this area was a smaller room with steel bars on the windows and a rather unusual looking machine with a type-writer key board which produced a strand of punched tape. I recall this well because on one occasion I accidentally pulled the covering sheet off this machine as I got down from my step ladder.

During your lunch break or on the completion of the whole job you were kept in the men's locker room. No walks in the grounds and once the transport arrived you were escorted back to the gate and that was it. Like many others who were employed by MPBW, I hated those visits to Gilnahirk wireless station."

And the warnings about security were not just idle threats and even minor transgressions were dealt with severely. I was given this account by a former member of staff.

"External security, that is access to CSOS Gilnahirk was the responsibility of a select group of retired Royal Ulster Constabulary officers. During the hours of day light, they would control the entry and exit from a small gatehouse at the main gate. During the hours of darkness, they would retreat into a security room just inside the main front entrance to the station building, Like everyone else their movement within the main building was restricted to the men's kitchen and toilets. Security within the remainder of the building was the responsibility of the duty officer at all times. He naturally was male and a full-time employee of GCHQ.

One married security officer began a relationship with a female friend who had no connections with the work of GCHQ and on occasions she would come to the station in the evenings and speak to her lover through the fence. On one occasion during the dark winters nights he brought that female friend into the gate house just inside the outer security fence at the main gate. Unfortunately, his failure to comply with the strict admittance procedures was observed and when he returned for duty the following evening he was confronted at the main gate by a total stranger who identified himself as a military police officer from Lisburn. The security officer was asked for his Gilnahirk pass and on handing it over was dismissed on the spot, the gate was then closed and locked and that was that. What appears to you and I as a bit over the top would have been considered differently by those in charge at GCHQ. Was this retired police officer going to be the victim of a "Honey Trap" which may have led eventually to a major breach of security at the station? During this period of time the Cold War was at its height and the KGB were capable of anything."

Thus if you are engaged as a telephonist at Gilnahirk wireless station and your job is to answer the switch board and route the calls and nothing else your knowledge of what goes on is greatly restricted. We can add another level to this restriction by warning this telephonist that he or she must not ask questions of others they work with directly or indirectly from other departments. This restriction is placed not only on the telephonist but on everyone working at Gilnahirk Wireless Station. You may ask questions of those in your department assuming they are doing the same job, anything more is potentially disastrous for your future in the Intelligence service. A further restriction is talking about your work to anyone not in your office or department. A failure to comply will lead to instant dismissal, arrest and a long period in prison for failing to keep the terms and conditions of the Official Secrets Act which you signed on day one of your employment.

Given this all enveloping blanket of secrecy it is not surprising that I cannot or, even if I could, would not reveal any detail about the work undertaken at Gilnahirk in the post war period. Although technology has advanced out of all recognition since the 70s there is a risk that such revelations could in some way harm the interests of this country and that is the last thing I would want to do.

In April 1956 Major Joe Banham was posted overseas to Singapore to be replaced by his replacement, a Mr. J.J. Hunter who had arrived in March 1956. Allowing for the break between the closing of the station in 1945 and the reopening in 1947 Joe Banham had served as commanding officer at Gilnahirk for almost sixteen years, an unusually long time as can be seen from to durations of the postings of those who succeeded him

In February 1960 Mr L.W. Jameson arrived to replace Hunter who moved on in March 1960.

Jameson was posted in September 1962 and was replaced by R. Saunders in October 1962. There appears to have been no period of transition on this occasion.

Saunders was posted in December 1964 and was replaced in that same month by D. Harrison.

Harrison was posted in April 1969 and was replaced by J.E. Walker who arrived in May 1969. Once again there appears to have been no period of transition.

Walker was posted in August 1972 the same month that his replacement W.M. Hicks arrives.

Hicks was posted in August 1974 of that year and his replacement was S. McNally. McNally would be the final officer in charge.

With the arrival of the digital age the face of communication was changing rapidly as UHF digital signals bounced between computers via satellites replaced HF signals bouncing of the ionosphere and RSA encryption. Computers allowed the use of incredibly secure ciphers such as RSA[1] public key encryption while spy satellites could invulnerably snoop on any countries communications.

Faced with these technological advances, the utility of listening stations such as Gilnahirk was rapidly diminishing and the station along with the site at Island Hill finally closed its doors in June 1978.

---

1   RSA public key encryption is named after Rivest, Shamir and Adleman from the USA who first publicly described the algorithm in a scientific paper in 1977 although it was subsequently revealed that two researchers working for GCHQ, James Ellis and Clifford Cocks, had independently come up with the same thing in 1973 but their work was buried behind a veil of secrecy for 24 years. The secret was finally revealed in December 1997 when Clifford Cocks delivered a public one month after James Ellis had died.

Internally the building was stripped bare leaving no trace of its former role. Handed back to the Northern Ireland Civil Service the building was used briefly by the Radio Interference Service followed by the Inland Revenue after which the building was allowed to fall into a state of neglect over a number of years before being placed on the market to be purchased by a local property developer.

In 2009 work began on the redevelopment of the site. The sixty-year-old government building with all its weaknesses of poor insulation, cost of heating and much more besides was raised to the ground and in its footprint twelve luxury apartments were constructed residing within their own private grounds with a gated entrance. To put the icing on the cake Castlereagh Borough Council agreed to name the new development Gilly Court Manor a fitting tribute to the contribution this location made to the work of Bletchley Park, and the Cold War.

Neglect, rebuild and a new purpose

During the very early days of my research I was warned that the possibility of finding anything on the achievements of Gilnahirk wireless station during WWII would be most unlikely given the deliberate attempts to conceal what went on there with the destruction of records at the end of the war.

Thankfully the luck of the Irish was to be on my side and over a period of time I was to uncover several fascinating stories. I share the following stories without for one moment suggesting they are in any way a comprehensive account of Gilnahirk's achievements nor even that they are definitive high points. Rather they are a peek under the veil to give a small flavour of why Gilnahirk along with its sister stations were so important to the Allied war effort.

The Bismarck.

First reports of a connection to the sinking of the Bismarck came from a member of the post war staff at Composite Signals Organisation station Gilnahirk. Alfie Allen a radio operator was one of the first to serve at the station when it went operational again in July 1947. He told me that one of a number of stories passed on from the wartime experiences of Major Joe Banham the officer in charge from 1940 to 1945 was that Gilnahirk had been involved with the operation which resulted in the sinking of the Bismark. However, while not wishing to doubt what Alfie had told me, I was reluctant to accept this until I had further supporting evidence.

Thankfully that supporting evidence was not long in coming. An interview with Kenneth Joseph Larkin, a Post Office teleprinter operator who served at Gilnahirk wireless station from 1940 to 1942 had a personnel experience to support what Alfie Allen had told me.

I quote from the interview.

"Gilnahirk was involved with some major marine event during my time, (May 1940 to October 1942). The sinking of some German vessel involved the Direction Finding site at Gilnahirk an aspect of the site I knew absolutely nothing about until this event took place. No further details were given to us about the sinking but the station did receive accreditation for the part it had played and this was passed on from Captain Joe Banham personally to the three watches. Shortly after this event I along with a number of others walked over to the Direction Finding site (i.e. the underground cabin) for the first and only time I was at Gilnahirk. I recall looking down into a hole in the ground where two men were sitting in front of some radio equipment. It was this direction finding aspect of the wireless station site that had made the valued contribution to the sinking of the German vessel."

We know from Britain's official wartime records concerning the final days of Bismarck's existence that her captain had played a game of cat and mouse with the Royal Navy. First being found by the Royal Navy and then being lost by the Royal Navy through a British error in plotting Bismarck's position from one or more of her radio transmissions which had been measured for compass bearings by the D/F process.

Unfortunately for me, Joseph Larkin did not mention the marine event by name, but all was not lost.

Some months later I made contact with Tony Banham, son of Major Joe Banham through a former Campbell College school friend of Tony. Having spoken to Tony at some length over the phone about his father's memories I invited Tony Banham to write everything down, sign it and send it to me please. This he did with pleasure and I now had the confirmation I needed for one of the notes read:-

In May 1941, stations a Cupar (Fife), Flowerdown, Land's End, Portrush (Northern Ireland), Scarborough and Wick (Scotland) gave fixes that together with radio finger-printing (RFP) helped track down the Bismarck. A total of twenty-three stations were involved.

Based on all that has been recovered I believe we can say with confidence that Gilnahirk (Northern Ireland) was one of those twenty-three.

Scharnhorst

Our next mention of a German Battleship comes from the wartime memories associated with Edgar Byrne a VI from the village of Clogher in County Tyrone. Edgar's son told me:-

"At war's end the visit of Lord Sandhurst to our home made a double impression on me: the threat of severe discipline if we misbehaved, and seeing his facial (duelling?) scar. Years later Dad told me that Lord Sandhurst had thanked him for all the good work and also said that he had picked up signals from the German Pocket Battleship Scharnhorst which helped with its location and destruction."

D-Day

When I had spoken to Tony Banham, son of Major Joe Banham I had also asked him to recall what if anything his father had said was Gilnahirk's single biggest contribution to the winning of world war two? The answer that came back loud and clear was D-Day.

To fully understand this answer, we should remember that as Major Banham's career with GCHQ continued after the war he would have become aware of events which at the time he like many others would not have been aware of. Banham would have known so much at his own level, but there was a much bigger picture and that he was not privy to. It was only through the passing of time that the contribution made by the Radio Security Service, of which Gilnahirk was a small element became clear.

Operation Overlord, the battleplan for the invasion of Normandy of which D-Day was a part, was the culmination of years of planning. Planning that was so methodical that nothing was left to chance but even so victory was not guaranteed and supreme Allied commander Dwight D Eisenhower had even prepared a speech in the event of failure.

The difficulties of mounting a seaborne invasion against a heavily defended coastline were well understood and it was realised that if the Germans concentrated their forces at the Allied landing sites it was this latter speech Eisenhower would be making.

As such a vital part of Overlord plan was to trick the Germans into thinking that the main invasion would occur at somewhere other than Normandy so as they would hold a significant element of their forces in reserve awaiting the main invasion rather than pouring them in to smash the Allied Normandy beachhead.

To achieve this deception the Allies conducted Operation Fortitude which included Fortitude North, a misinformation campaign using fake radio traffic to lead the Germans into expecting an attack on Norway and Fortitude South, a major deception designed to fool the Germans into believing that the landings would take place at Pas de Calais in July.

As I explained earlier in this book, from the earliest days of the war British Intelligence had largely conquered the espionage threat posed by the Abwher through operations such as the Double Cross program. The extent of this victory was such that, for most of the war, the Abwher was receiving what it assumed to be a stream high grade intelligence from its agents in Britain when what it was actually getting was information from British Intelligence designed to shape German thinking to the advantage of the Allies.

However for such an operation to be successful it was not enough to simply feed mis-information to the Germans – the Allies had to know how the Germans were reacting to it and this is where the RSS contributed a most vital role.

By being able to tap into the Abwher communications network the RSS were able to advise the Allied commanders what the Germans actually thought was happening which gave the instigators of Operation Fortitude the opportunity to present the German war machine with precisely the evidence required to lead it to entirely the wrong conclusion.

This insight into German thinking was a keystone in the success of Operation Fortitude and success it was. Even when the Allied beach heads were getting established in Normandy Hitler refused his generals permission to release the reserves bottled up at Pas de Calais waiting for and invasion that never came.

A few years ago I was granted an insight into how closely wireless Station No 4 (Gilnahirk) was involved with all this by a most unusual source. It is not an official document marked secret, but a plain piece of pink card the size of a standard post card given to Ulsterman Sgt Arthur Irwin by fellow signalman George Cooper.

One of 73 QSL cards collected by Arthur Irwin from fellow amateurs, recruited as VIs.

Of Ivor and Mary we've heard quite a lot,
Of Patrick and Harry and Willie,
Of Violet and also the one that is known as Bertie at Gilly.
When at long last I leave these shores behind,
And say my farewell to Gilly,
The One I shall think of most of all,
Is Bertie not Willie.
George Cooper 8/11/1943

What at first appears to be a short poem, an innocent collection of boys and girl's names is in fact a remarkable piece of documentation the meaning of which only became clear when I discovered another document in the archives at Kew, London. This document detailing the British Code Names for the various German Abwehr regions revealed what George Cooper was alluding to in his poem – that the RSS Operators at Gilnahirk were intercepting and recording the Abwher stations right across the continent.

Bertie (BERLIN) was group two of the Abwehr.

Willie (Wiesbaden) was group three.

Ivor (Italian) was group eight.

Patrick (Paris) was group five.

Violet, (Vienna) was group seven.

Harry was group one of the Abwehr services located near Hamburg.

Mary is one that remains a mystery.

The term "Gilly" is the adopted wartime nickname of the Gilnahirk wireless station site and it comes from the Telex abbreviation which was used to address or identify any messages from Gilnahirk. (In many ways similar to a Telephone Number)

Here was the proof that the most westerly of all the RSS regions within the British Isles was doing its bit for King and Country. German Abwehr messages transmitted over one thousand miles away were being captured and recorded by the watches at station No 4 (Gilnahirk).

So on reflection Major Joe Banham's assessment that D-Day was Gilnahirk's greatest success was concluded from everything that the civilian and military staff of Gilnahirk wireless station had achieved. An interception that on paper was simply a collection of letters or numbers gave our commanders knowledge and understanding that put together with other sources of intelligence allowed us to see a

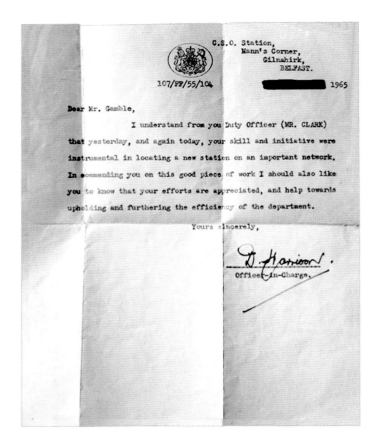

C.S.O. Station,
Mann's Corner,
Gilnahirk,
BELFAST.

107/FF/55/104   1965

Dear Mr. Gamble,

I understand from you Duty Officer (MR. CLARK)
that yesterday, and again today, your skill and initiative were
instrumental in locating a new station on an important network.
In commending you on this good piece of work I should also like
you to know that your efforts are appreciated, and help towards
upholding and furthering the efficiency of the department.

Yours sincerely,

D. Harison.
Officer-In-Charge.

much bigger picture. D-Day was indeed the ultimate success after hours, days, weeks and years of listening and interception.

When I began my research into the history and purpose of Gilnahirk Wireless Station I was advised that research into the Cold War operations and duties of Gilnahirk was a door I should leave firmly closed. The station has been operational for approximately thirty-six years but with this advice in mind my research into the operations at Gilnahirk has been limited to only the first five of those years.

However sometimes, even though not seeking information on the Cold War period I would be given information or ducuments from the time. On one such occasion I was given the letter on the left by the widow of Mr John Gamble former radio operator at Gilnahirk. It confirms that at the height of the Cold War CSOS Gilnahirk was still quietly contributing at the leading edge of the UK's security.

A t the end of WWII the full-time radio operators at Station No 4 received their standard issue medals. As for the Post Office staff who finished in September 1942 I have no idea what if anything they received. As for the Voluntary Interceptor he would receive a letter of thanks from Col. Maltby OIC of the Radio Security Service, plus a certificate recording his name and years of service signed by Sir Herbert Creely of the war office.

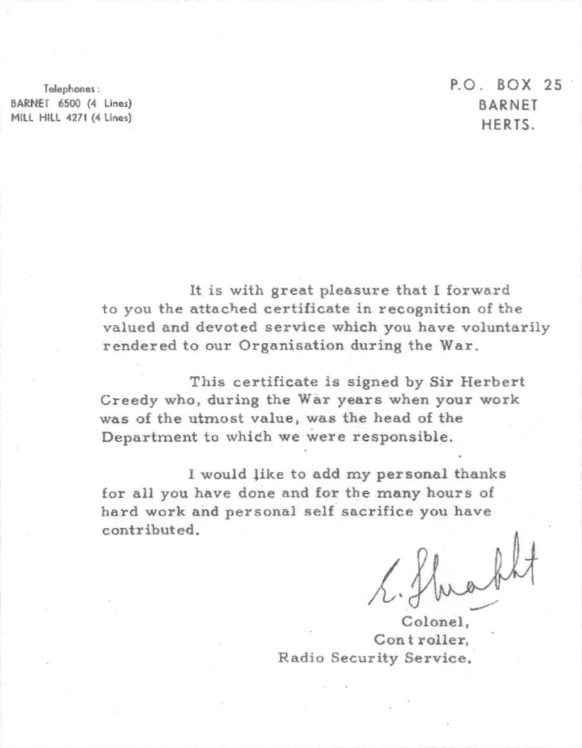

Telephones :
BARNET 6500 (4 Lines)
MILL HILL 4271 (4 Lines)

P.O. BOX 25
BARNET
HERTS.

It is with great pleasure that I forward to you the attached certificate in recognition of the valued and devoted service which you have voluntarily rendered to our Organisation during the War.

This certificate is signed by Sir Herbert Creedy who, during the War years when your work was of the utmost value, was the head of the Department to which we were responsible.

I would like to add my personal thanks for all you have done and for the many hours of hard work and personal self sacrifice you have contributed.

Colonel,
Controller,
Radio Security Service.

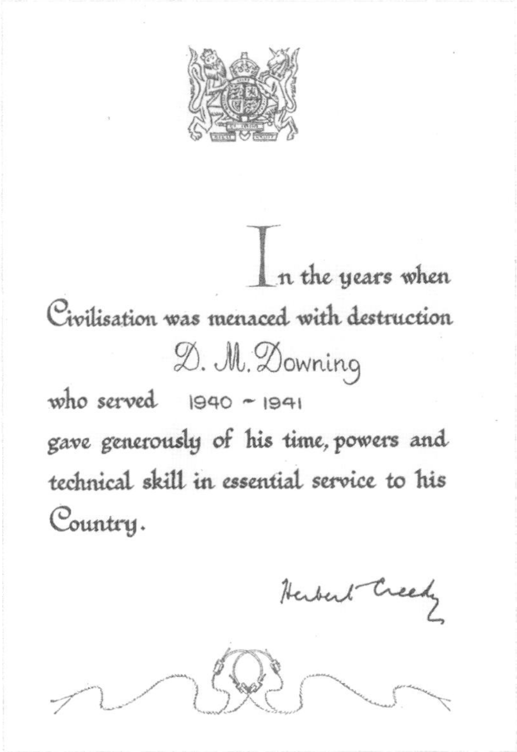

I n the years when Civilisation was menaced with destruction D. M. Downing who served 1940 ~ 1941 gave generously of his time, powers and technical skill in essential service to his Country.

Herbert Creedy

Left: Maltby's letter
Right: Dr Des Downing's Certificate of service.

1946 New Year's Honour's List

Among those awarded the British Empire Medal at this time was one Voluntary Interceptor from each of the nine RSS regions within the United Kingdom. In Northern Ireland that award was given to John Nelson Smith, (GI 5QX). The award was hidden behind services to the Royal Observer Crops as this was the uniform the VIs in England, Scotland and Wales wore during WWII. In Northern Ireland our VIs wore the Home Guard Uniform. Mention of this award was not recorded within the lists published in the local Northern Ireland Press, i.e. *The Belfast Telegraph*, *The News Letter* and others. Despite my best efforts to track this medal down, John and his wife appear to have had no family and as a result the whereabouts of the medal today are unknown.

2009

In 2009 the Government of the day announced the award of the Bletchley Badge and Certificate for all those who had served at Bletchley Park and the out Stations during WWII. In order the qualify the veteran had to be alive and well on the 1st July 2009. There would be no exceptions only the living would receive a badge.

However, to the best of my knowledge, by 2009 there were no surviving wartime VIs from Northern Ireland. When I raised this with the Bletchley Park Trust, a decision was taken to send

a Bletchley Badge and a Certificate signed by Prime Minister David Cameron to the Somme Museum on behalf of all the Northern Ireland Voluntary Interceptors.

As for those who were no longer with us they would have their names entered into the Veterans Register which was to be held by the

Bletchley Park Trust assuming someone knew of their service with the work of Bletchley Park.

Finally, in 2011 Her Majesty Queen Elizabeth II unveiled a Caithness stone memorial within the grounds of Bletchley Park to the Out Stations that supported the work of Bletchley Park.

Among the names on this memorial was that of Gilnahirk.

The Inscription:–

"We Also Served"

Appendix 1: Notes on the Detection of Illicit Wireless 1940

Below is the transcript of a document I was given by Major Joe Banham's son, Tony, during my research. Although the document is subject to Crown Copyright, it is transcribed here with the kind permission of the Director GCHQ. The document gives a wonderful insight into the thinking and technology of the time.

GENERAL INSTRUCTIONS.

The following instructions are issued as a result of experience, suggestion, and enquires in peace and war, up to date.

OBJECT OF THE ORGANISATION

The object is to intercept, locate and close down, illicit wireless stations operated either by enemy agents within the United Kingdom or by persons not necessarily enemy agents operating transmitting stations without being licensed to do so under Defence Regulations 1939.

SECRET   Copy No. 21
(Not for publication – Crown copyright reserved)

NOTES ON THE
DETECTION OF
ILLICIT WIRELESS
1940

NOTES ON THE DETECTION OF ILLICIT WIRELESS

By Lt.-Colonel Adrain Simpson, C.M.G, R.E., A.M.I.E.E., Late Deputy Managing Director, Maroni's Wireless Telegraph Co. Ltd., and Director of Wireless Telegraphs to the Government of India.

NOTES ON THE DETECTION OF ILLICIT WIRELESS

1. It is hardly necessary to emphasise that these notes are highly confidential and that the illicit use of wireless transmitting apparatus is an offence against No 8 of the Defence Regulations 1939.

2. In the last war the science of wireless was comparatively speaking in its infancy and it would have been quite impossible for any enemy agent to have attempted to make use of wireless as a method of secret communication, with the hope of success. He would have been located by our Direction Finding Stations within a matter of minutes and would have been rounded up and under lock and key with a matter of hours.

3. One case actually occurred in 1918 when a small but over enthusiastic section of Territorials with more zeal than discretion, proceeded to carry out a night practice with some captured German apparatus near Hampton Court. They were located and rounded up by a squadron of cavalry within three quarters of an hour, and spent an uncomfortable night in the guard room before their bona – fides were established.

4. The position to-day is very different. The science of wireless transmission has developed at such a phenomenal rate that the practical difficulties of detecting a skilled agent have increased out of all proportion.

5. The reason for this is simple. In the last war we had to deal only with medium and long waves, which could be D.F.'d with considerable accuracy and rapidity. Not only this, but also their employment entailed much greater power and larger aerials, a fact which would have rendered an agent who might have wished to establish an illicit station far more liable to detection by an casual observer than is the case to-day.

6. Mainly owing to the introduction of short waves, the whole problem has become an exceedingly complex one, owing partly to the vast increase in the number of wave lengths available, and the enormous number of stations of all nationalities operating on the ether at all times of the day and night, there by tending to cloak an irregular or illicit transmission on low power and partly owing to the long ranges which can be obtained with a very small expenditure of energy, coupled with possible complications such as the use of single side band transmission. And last but not least the exceedingly small dimensions of the apparatus, which need not occupy a space much greater than say a large sized dictionary, or a 3lb biscuit tin.

7. Add to this the facts that short waves are far more difficult to D.F. with rapidity and accuracy, that they are seriously interfered with by physical objects such as ballon barrages, overhead trolley bus wires, even lamp-posts and trees, etc., that an outside and therefore visible aerial is no longer necessary and some idea will be obtained of the extreme complexity of the problem before us.

8. In notes of this kind, a certain number of technical references are unavoidable and whilst some readers are first-rate radio experts, others have not had the advantage (or disadvantage) of an extensive training in wireless and

technicalities will therefore be avoided as much as possible.

9. As already pointed out the present day wireless transmission problem is a very complex one, but fortunately, from the particular aspect from which we are called upon to view the question, it may be somewhat narrowed down, if we are prepared to assume, as we can reasonably do, that, as a general rule:-

(a) Only low power will be employed;

(b) Bulky or intricate apparatus will be involved;

(c) Complicated aerial systems will not be used owing to the ease with which they can be spotted.

(d) Only continuous waves will be employed;

(e) Morse keying at hand speed will in all probability be favoured in preference to telephony, which for any given range, requires more power and is therefore more likely to be detected.

10. If we accept the above premises we are able to arrive at certain general conclusions; 'general' because while wireless waves no doubt obey certain rigid laws, our knowledge of these laws is unfortunately far from perfect and we can only draw inferences, which are true in the majority of cases.

11. As you all know, wireless transmitters send out what for the sake of convenience may be described as a composite wave, which for practical purposes can be resolved into two components, namely the ground ray and the reflected ray.

12. The ground ray, as its name implies, tends to follow the curvature of the earth. In the case of low power short wave stations, as its intensity is small, it is rapidly damped out and can only be hard at comparatively short distances. This distance depends largely on the physical properties of the earth's surface. For instance, the ground ray will carry much further over sea than it will over land.

13. The so-called reflected ray on the other hand, leaves the transmitting aerial at an abrupt angle, travels upwards until it meets a series of conducting layers, known as the ionosphere, from one or other of which it is reflected downwards, coming to earth again over an area, the nearest part of which may be several hundred or even thousand miles from the point of transmission. This distance in miles between the point of transmission and the line at which the reflected wave returns to the earth's surface is termed the skip distance and it should be remembered that this skip distance tends to increase as the wavelength decreases.

14 Within the skip signals may or may not be audible. The under surface of the ionosphere is not smooth and some scattered reflections may come back into the skip area. In general, it is not possible to obtain good D.F. bearings on transmitting stations when the D.F. station is within this skip.

15. Very short waves are not reflected by the ionosphere, but pass through it and are lost in space. Such wavelengths, however, can only be used in a manner somewhat similar to that in which visual lamps or helio signalling can be used, i.e., the path between sender and receiver must be fairly clear of optical obstructions.

16. Without entering into a detailed technical discussion as to the reasons which have led to the following conclusions, it is fairly safe to say that wavelengths of 6 metres and under are not likely to be used in the present state of development, since waves of this order would be liable to atmospheric refraction and they would not be suitable for reliable communications, except at very short ranges.

17. Wavelengths of the order of 7 to 14 meters might well be employed for communications across the North Sea, say from the English to the Dutch or Belgian coast, on the assumption that both the transmitting as well as the receiving stations are situated right on the coast. A few miles of land intervening on either side would necessitate the use of longer waves. These wavelengths will certainly require to be watched for back radiation over the land could be made extremely weak and our permanent D.F. stations would probably hear nothing whatever. The signals would, however, be picked up locally by and trained observer with a suitable receiver.

18 Wavelengths of 15 to 20 metres are very suitable for regular reliable ground ray communication from coast to coast. There should be no marked fading between say, 15 and 20 metres at any time and these wavelengths must be closely watched by local observers, as it is more than probable that signals on these frequencies would only be audible in the vicinity of the transmitter.

19. Ground ray communication on wavelengths of the order of 20 to 70 metres is not likely to be used as this band would almost certainly suffer from sever fading during the daytime.

On the other hand, this wave band (20 to0 70 metres) is extremely important for reflected or ionosphere ray communications.

20. As we go up the scale of wavelengths however the value of the ground ray for communication purposes commences to predominate and speaking very roughly, one may say the "skip" effect ceases to have any practical value for reliable communication for wavelengths of 120 metres and upwards and the ground ray will then become the predominant factor.

IONOSPHERE OR REFLECTED RAY COMMUNICATION

21. As just indicated, the wave band 20 to 70 metres is extremely important for reflected ray communications, particularly for distances such as we are called upon to envisage – that is to say from England to Germany and Central Europe.

22. The shortest wave reliably received by reflection from the ionosphere will depend on the time of day or night, season, sunspot cycle and other factors which we need not consider here. Suffice it to say that during the winter season the figure will be approximately 25 metres during the day and is very seldom ever likely to be less than 20 metres at any time. (On disturbed days the figure may be 40 to 50 metres.) At night the shortest wave for normal reflection will increase probably reaching values of 60 to 70 metres.

23. Assuming therefore an efficient receiving station somewhere in Germany, it should be quite possible to select a suitable wavelength , having regard to range and seasonal conditions, which would give a regular reliable service. If such a station were to be established in a carefully chosen locality in this country, it would very likely not be heard at all at our permanent interception and D.F. stations. The apparatus required would occupy very little space and only a comparatively small aerial would be necessary. The station could be situated in the centre of a densely populated area, or alternatively it might well be installed in a small car with a portable aerial which could be fixed to a convenient tree or chimney. Indeed, on the shorter wave 20 to 60 metres quite a small aerial is all that is necessary. A vertical rod 12ft long, attachable to the car or even a good car radio fixed aerial would be sufficient.

GROUND RAY

24. We will now leave the skip effect and come back to our friend the ground ray, for as already pointed out, as we increase our wavelength and reflected rays from the ionosphere will tend to become weaker, particularly during the daytime, as compared with the ground rays over the normal communication ranges for whch these wave lengths are used. Moreover, the apparatus tends to become considerably more bulky, a larger amount of primary energy is required, thereby rendering the signals easier to detect, while the aerial becomes correspondingly bigger and more difficult to hide.

25. Generally speaking, therefore it is unlikely that wavelengths of over say 120 metres will be used for ordinary illicit communication – and by that is meant the sort of communication that an enemy agent would endeavour to establish for the purpose of sending information out of this country.

26. It is not wished to convey by this statement that the enemy will not try to use medium and long waves – in fact, we have definite indications that he will do so for special purposes. All that is suggested is that short waves, low power, and a small aerial are more likely to be used by the gentleman who wants to hide himself in a thickly populated area. This is a fair assumption because an agent who wants to send out information, which in turn argues a regular scheduled service, will not want to increase his own difficulties and consequently the risk of discovery, by installing a medium or long wave station somewhere out in the wilds to which he would have to convey his information before he could dispatch it.

27. There is, however, one important exception – the so called illicit beacon station – and we may as well deal with this at once. Beacon stations, as you probably know are wireless transmitters designed to send out a characteristic signal – usually of a repetitive nature – which ast as navigational aids to aeroplanes fitted with direction finding apparatus. Such a station, secretly installed in one of our large manufacturing towns or near an important military objective, would, if it were not detected, enable enemy planes to fly straight to their objective. Alternatively, such a station erected near the coast or on a vessel within the three mile limit would furnish and excellent land fall or jumping off point for attacking aircraft.

28. To this you will probably reply: "Here! Wait a minute you told us just now that medium and long wave stations are much more easily detected because they have to use more power and can therefore be more easily located by our D.F. stations and because the apparatus and aerials are necessarily larger and can be more easily spotted. Furthermore, a beacon station to be of maximum value must be fairly near its target which would in most cases be in a thickly populated area. Why then should they use such stations and so increase the risk of discovery?" The answer is that they cannot help themselves, at any rate in the present state of development. Owing to the high noise level in an aeroplane, fairly powerful signals are required if they are to be received at a sufficiently long range to be of practical navigational value to the plane flying at a speed of anything from 200 to 300 miles an hour.

29. For reasons which it is unnecessary to enter into here, it may be said that any station which the Germans are likely to have erected for this purpose will, at any rate for the present, work on a wavelength of not less than 300 metres and not more than 1,750 metres; and whilst admittedly the risk of location and detection is much greater than that of a low power short wave station, it is never the less not so great as would at first appear, if you consider the circumstances. Assume that an agent knows his job and can find , let us say, an old disused factory with a medium-sized chimney stack in which to hide her aerial, or alternatively a private house with a good television aerial on the roof (the down leads of

a television aerial would, suitably connected, make a very efficient transmitting aerial for this purpose) situated near the target and on the correct line of approach. Even a broadcast receiver aerial can be used. A good aerial for the purpose would be a long broadcast aerial, attached to a high tree or chimney top, broken by an insulator to comply with the P.M.G.'s Regulations limiting the active length to 100ft; for the purpose of illicit transmission this insulator could easily be bridged over in a way which would be invisible from the ground.

30. All he has to do now is to get his transmitter installed, which he can test out on a non-radiating closed circuit aerial and he can now sit down quietly and wait for zero hour and nobody any the wiser. When a raid is signalled on that particular objective, and there are a hundred ways of doing this, all he need do is switch on his transmitter, operated by an automatic device which will repeat a pre-arranged signal and then retire quietly to the nearest dug-out. In effect this means that the beacon will only be on the air for perhaps 15 or 20 minutes at the outside and although the D.F. stations may succeed in locating the area it is going to be an extremely difficult job, especially in a black out, to locate the actual site.

31. The importance of dealing with the beacon problem will naturally be appreciated, as all our elaborate arrangements for plunging the country into Stygian darkness will not be of very much avail if the enemy is to be allowed to erect wireless beacons in or near our big cities, which in these circumstances would remain, from a wireless point of view, almost as brightly illuminated as they are in peace time. Having reached this stage let us now try to summarise the position and see where it is leading us.

32. We can conveniently summarise the position by saying that there are four main forms of illicit transmission for which we have to keep watch:-
(i) The beacon gentleman operating on from 300 to 1,750 metres.
(ii) The agent whose duty is to warn the enemy when our own Bombing squadrons are taking the air.
(iii) The Intelligence agent whose duty it is to collect information and convey it to the other side.
(iv) The agent whose duty it, may be to communicate from the shore to submarines and sea-going craft.

33. Let us take these in order:-
(i) Beacon stations, - Owing to the wavelength employed and the fact that more power is necessary to obtain the requisite range, these stations will probably be picked up at once by our interception and D.F. stations, who will be able to give us the approximate area where the station is located, but we shall be lucky if our Regional G.P.O. vans (which form part of the technical organisation) are able to locate the actual premises from which the transmission is taking place – bearing in mind that they may have to operate during a complete black-out, that the station will only be on the air for a few minutes at a time and will not be heard again till the occasion of the next raid or the next wave of attack. In other words, it will come down in the end to a question of local initiative and organised local intelligence, assisted perhaps by technical experts and specialised apparatus, before the station can be finally localised and put out of action. It is not suggested that the machinery of our technical organisation would not be able to locate the station too, if left to itself, but it is suggested that the desired result will be brought about very much more rapidly if local knowledge and intelligence is brought to bear. And in such circumstances the time element is vital, as it may well mean the saving of many lives as well as the preservation of valuable property.
(ii) Air raid warnings conveyed to the enemy – Here again the prevention of leakage of information to the enemy must mean the preservation of valuable lives and machines and in as much as short waves (probably of the order of 20 to 70 metres) are almost certain to be used to take advantage of the skip effect, it follows that the first intimation of the existence of such stations will very often come as a result of local observation.
(iii) Leakage of general information – Here again the same remarks apply, only even more so, because it is highly probable that the station will be situated in a densely populated district, where the ground wave, which is all we have to warn us of the presence of the station, will probably not be audible over a radius of more than ten miles, if as much.
(iv) Shore to ship – In this case we again may have to rely on local observation to tell us that an illicit station is working in our midst and as we may be dealing here with waves of the order of say 20 metres down to 5 or even 3 metres with a station situated very near the coast and very little back radiation from our friend the ground ray, we shall have to rely to a very large extent, if not entirely, on local information to enable the technical machinery of the War Office and the G.P.O. (that is to say the whole system of D.F. stations, interception stations and mobile vans) requires to be supplemented and assisted by a body of trained observers as well as an organised system of local intelligence to examine and co-ordinate the information collected.

34. It is in this duty – one of paramount importance – the collection and co-ordination of local intelligence – without which the technical organisation cannot hope to succeed –

that the Police are now being asked to assist us. And when it is explained that ultimate success will depend to something like 80 per cent, on organised intelligence and 20 per cent, on technical machinery, you will appreciate the vital importance of the work you are being asked to undertake. Resourcefulness, a keen power of observation and unlimited patience are the necessary ingredients of success. Two examples may be given; - In more than one instance it was observed that a certain light circuit was nearly resonant and became incandescent each time the key of the transmitter closed. In another instance quiet enquires into certain of the many motor repair shops, scattered over the countryside, with very little apparent business and installations inconsistent with their visible needs, have led to surprising results.

35. It is for this reason and for the benefit of those readers who are not acquainted with the technical aspect of the problem that an attempt has been made to explain in general terms the salient features of the problem, for it the Police are to help in this very important work it is necessary to have a clear understanding of what that problem is.

36. To seek an analogy, the whole business is rather like a shooting party to which the host has invited a number of guns.
The partridges or pheasants, as the case
may be, are our illicit birds.
The guns represent our technical organisation
and if you like the host is the Government.
The vans are, if you please, the beaters; the observers
are the dogs, and the Police the keepers.
True, the party may go out with a number of beaters and if they are lucky they may put up a few coveys, but on the other hand, they may walk over the birds or there may even be no birds at all on the bit of a shoot. If, on the other hand, the host is a wise man he has so organised his shoot that beaters have been over the ground beforehand with the dogs – they have collected all the intelligence available as to where the birds are and are able to place the beaters to the best advantage.

37. So much for the problem itself. Now as to its solution.
The first problem is to cover the country as
far as possible with a 24hr watch.
This means forming an observer corps of trained listeners to supplement any organised listening that can be undertaken by the Police, and obviously from their intimate local knowledge, the Police are far and away the best judges as to the qualifications and character of any individuals in the district who are prepared to off their services.
As far as possible men should be chosen who are ex-Fighting

Service, Mercantile Marine, or G.P.O. operators with a good knowledge of Morse, or who have made radio their hobby in peace time. Of the latter, the men who have belonged to purely listening societies may possibly be of more value than the average member of the R.S.G.B. who, as a rule, is prone to have been more interested in using his own transmitting set than in listening to others. However this may be – and it is only put forward as a suggestion – the thing is to get together a corps of listeners or observers who are accustomed to listening in and who, after a short time, will be capable of discriminating between various types of transmission and of recognising an unusual or suspicious signals as soon as they occur. Whilst many men will be found to be in possession of receiving sets well adapted for the purpose, others will have to be supplied with sets on loan. All listeners will have to be supplied with log-forms on which to report the results of their work.

38. It is proposed to divide the whole country into nine regions and to place an Army Officer of the Radio Security Service (M.I.8, W.O.), in wireless charge of each region.
(i) He will be responsible for the selection of civilian observers, having regard to their character, reliability and qualifications.
(ii) He will see that all listeners, whether members of the Force or civilians, are supplied with special forms for logging intercepts, showing call signs, frequency, nature of signals, etc., etc.
(iii) He will arrange for the transmission of one copy direct to the H.Q. of the R.S.S. with the least possible delay, anything of a suspicious nature being forwarded by telephone, in code if necessary, or by tele-printer if available.
(iv) Any deductions or suggestions which the Officer i/c District is able to make will be forwarded in the form of a report in duplicate for instructions as to what action (if any) is to be taken.
(v) He will arrange for the calibration of all receiving sets in his district.
(vi) He will endeavour to arrange for the receipt of reports from trustworthy dealers regarding any unusual enquires or sales of parts of transmitting apparatus, power valves, X-ray or electro – therapeutic apparatus, or other information of a suspicious nature.
(vii) He should endeavour to obtain from local electricity supply companies reports of an unusual consumption of current.
(viii) He should have access to all reports from informers in the district regarding individuals suspected of illicit transmitting. Such reports are now being forwarded by *Chief Constables to the Director of Security Services (D.S.S.), and this should

continue to be done, but where technical details are available, such as frequency, call sign, etc., etc., such information should be communicated immediately to O. i/c Region, R.S.S. *(In Northern Ireland; The Inspector General, R.U.C.)

(ix) He will be furnished with a complete list, containing names and addresses, of all individuals in his district who have held transmitting licences in peace time, as well as a list of any exemptions from the closing down order.

(x) He will be responsible for the issue of any wireless instructions which it may be necessary to circulate from time to time.

(xi) He will arrange for watches to be kept in his Region, on frequencies to be laid down, having regard to the number of men available and the individual apparatus in their possession.

(xii) Generally speaking he will act as wireless intelligence officer and be responsible for the Region of which he is Officer i/c.

(xiii) In suspected cases of illicit transmitters and even in cases where transmission is actually taking place no direct police action should ever be taken without previous reference to the D.S.S. The only exception to this rule is where an obvious beacon has been located, or is some other very urgent and special circumstances where a Police Officer and/or the Officer i/c Region may be called upon to exercise his own initiative. The reason for this will be readily appreciated by the Police, for it is analogous to the case of keeping a criminal under observation instead of arresting out of hand, in order to find out with whom he is associating. It is the same thing with wireless – we can sometimes find out much more by letting him go on for a time so as to ascertain which whom he is corresponding and if we are lucky, what he is saying. *Added by G.G. Busby.

39. It goes without saying that the Police will assist the R.O. in the exercise of his duties by informing him of all suspicious cases of a wireless character, in addition to forwarding their official report to the D.S.S. as hereto fore.

40. In cases where a search is decided upon by the D.S.S. it is the duty of the R.O. to obtain and provide the Police with any technical assistance which may be required.

41. At this juncture let us suppose we have a had a bit of luck – that we have located one of these gentlemen and have decided to raid the premises.
To start with this can be done either under No. 88a(1) of the Defence Regulations (Search Warrant), or if the case is urgent under No. 88A(2) (Superintendents' Authority0. In both cases the suspected offence is against

No. 8 of the Regulations dealing with the possession of illicit wireless transmitting apparatus or parts thereof.

42. In the event of an offence against the Regulations being established as a result of the raid, the individual or individuals concerned should be arrested and a full repost sent to the D.S.S. immediately. No charge should be made pending receipt of further instructions from the D.S.S.

43. In making a search of this nature it is of the utmost importance that the Police Officer conduction the charge should be a radio expert or that he should be accompanied by someone with the necessary expert knowledge. An d again, it is extremely important that the suspect should not have the slightest inkling that he is under observations during the preliminary stages, for it would only be the work of a few minutes to take the whole bag of trick out into the garden and bury it. You might search till the cows came home and find not traces. The importance of both these points cannot possibly be overstated, because, as has already been pointed out, the apparatus you are looking for may, in the case of a short wave set, i.e. not bigger that a good sized dictionary, or about the size of an ordinary office filing tray.

44. It is more than probable that both the aerial and the apparatus may be installed between the ceiling of a flat and the floor of the flat above and all the operator has to do whenever he wishes to work the set is to plug his key into what appears to be an ordinary lighting point, switch on the current and proceed to transmit. This will give some idea of the thoroughness with which a search of this kind has to be conducted whenever the evidence justifies it.

45. And this is one more reason for going slow in the majority of cases before action is taken, as it is necessary to be pretty sure of one's facts before going in and pulling a man's home to pieces. Preliminary discreet enquiries will often decide whether the individual, from his previous history and qualifications is likely to have a transmitter, or be able to work one. But as you will have observed, the enquiries must be very discreet.

46. However, having decided to raid the premises and obtained the blessing of the D.S.S. and the necessary warrant (say a Superintendents' Authority), what is the best way to do it? The first thing to decide is when to enter. And this is very important. It is best to avoid entering when the suspect is at work because if he is actually transmitting he may be able to send a danger signal intimation that he has been caught, which would nullify the possibility of using him and his set if de elected to turn King's Evidence.

47. And here let a word of warning be added. The police Officer in charge of the investigation should make such arrangements

as will enable him to swear on oath that no person left the premises during the interval between the cessation of transmission, i.e., between the moment when signals ceased and his entry into the house, otherwise the suspect may escape under No. 8 (2) of the Defence Regulations 1939, by swearing that some third person was committing the offence without his knowledge. In such a case even a Dictaphone record of the actual signals might fail to secure a conviction if it could not be sworn hat no person had quitted the premises.

48. Now let us imagine we have gained access to the premises. What are we going to look for? Unless the man is a lunatic or a complete fool at his job, we are certainly not going to see a neat little transmitting set laid out on the sitting room table with key complete and an obvious di-pole aerial on the roof. We will in all probability see nothing but an innocent receiving set. First of all we must examine that set and make sure that it is a receiver. The next thing to do is to search thoroughly the premises, including the furniture, fireplaces and all papers and correspondence. The presence of a calibration chart or an invoice for a quartz crystal, of a transmitting key, a microphone, or a pair of headphone (he is unlikely to use a loud speaker for reception from the other side in order to avoid drawing attention to himself), or a scrap of coded message may give the whole show away. An then lastly, if you are still convinced that there is a transmitter somewhere, set t to and trace to its source every bit of electrical wiring in the house, even if it means pulling up the floor boards to do so. And don't forget the garage and car if there is one. If nothing if found after this, the only thing to do is to apologise as sweetly as possible and go home.

BORDER LINE CASES

49. A word should now be said regarding the type of case with which all are familiar – the case which, owing to a lack of definite evidence, scarcely seems to justify the issue of a search warrant and a police examination of the premises. In normal times one might be inclined to adopt one of the following courses:-

(a) Ask the Police to be good enough to send a Police Officer possessing the necessary radio knowledge to interview the person in question; or

(b) Ask the G.P.O. to send a Radio Interference Officer, ostensibly to examine the suspect's licence and apparatus on the grounds of an alleged report of interference, but in reality to have an excuse to examine the premises.

(c) Arrange for an excuse to enter the premises under No 85 (1) (B) of the Defence Regulations, ("Land" includes

buildings: see No 100 of the Defence Regulations.)

50. Cases of this kind are occurring daily in which, due to ignorance or a too vivid imagination on the part of the informant, some perfectly innocent and respectable individual is accused of transmitting without a licence and since the war broke out, a very large number of perfectly innocent cases have been satisfactorily disposed of in one or another of the above mentioned ways without giving offence or causing inconvenience to the individual in question.

51. Actually, none of the these methods is satisfactory, for, in one or two cases, objection to entry into the premises has been encountered (as to which see No. 82 of the Defence Regulations), and time has been lost in obtaining the necessary authority, thereby affording ample opportunity for the disposal of incrimination evidence before further action could be taken. Owing to the extremely small space occupied by modern low power short wave transmitting apparatus, all evidence of its existence can easily be cleared away in a matter of a few minutes, and therefore it is essential to devise some modus operandi to meet this point and which, at the same time, will cause a minimum of inconvenience or offence to the individual in question.

52. To overcome the difficulty it is recommended that in such cases the suspect should be visited, of course without an previous warning, by a Police Officer, accompanied by a G.P.O. Radio Interference Officer, ostensibly to investigate an alleged complaint of interference and that the Police Officer should go armed with a Superintendent's Authority under No 88 a (2) of the Defence Regulations 1989, which should not, however, be produced or used unless objection is raised to entry, or unless after entry has been effected, evidence is forthcoming which, in the opinion of the Police Officer and / or the G.P.O. Officer, justifies a detailed and exhaustive search of the premises.

53. When carrying out a search, there is one other aspect of illicit transmission which must not be lost sight of. It is all the more important as it is not covered by the present regulations, although it is believed that steps are being taken to amend them. The reference is to the question of radiation from diathermic apparatus, X-ray equipment and the like. Unfortunately, for our point of view, one cannot prevent medical men, dentists and others, from possessing equipment which forms part of their regular business, but at the same time it must be borne in mind that in the wrong hands such equipment is a potential danger, as it can be transformed into a wireless transmitter in a few minutes.

54. Finally, there is the question of infra-red ray radiation

and that question has arisen as to whether powers should not be taken to limit this as well.

An infra-red beam transmitter can easily be made up from a suitable type of focussing electric torch, fitted with a screen cutting off visual rays and passing infra-red. Suitable screens are sold by many photographic dealers and in fact a thin sheet of ebonite makes an excellent filter.

An ordinary torch gives strong infra-red emanations, which can be picked up by a simple and lightweight detector attached to an aeroplane, actuated by one of the types of photo-electric cells particularly sensitive in the infra – red region. Conditions during a "black-out" are, of course, very suitable for the operation of such a device, and the operator would be very difficult to locate from the ground.

55 And now let a warning be given of a few common pitfalls to avoid.

In times like these, whey spy fever is rampant, every report while it must be investigated, should be treated with the utmost reserve, the informer's evidence carefully sifted and his bona fides established.

Recent experience has shown that a large majority of informers reports are due to over-zealousness or to too vivid an imagination and in some cases to malice.

His or her grounds of suspicion must be carefully examined and wherever possible information on the following points elicited by questioning:-

(a) If seen, what did the apparatus look like, and in what respects did it appear to differ from an ordinary receiver?

(b) If signals are alleged to have been intercepted, it is important to know:

    (i)   When heard – time and date?

    (ii) On how many occasions?

    (iii) Telephony or Morse? Text, if possible.

    (iv) What language?

    (v) Wavelength (if known)? If not known was it near and other station on the scale?

    (vi) Call signs used (if any)?

    (vii) Relative loudness of signals?

    (viii) What make of receiver was being used, when the suspected signals were heard and what kind of receiving aerial?

56. Another common pitfall, which is a frequent source of genuine error, is to be found in the report by an informer that Mr X has been heard transmitting – whereas Mr X has probably never seen a transmitter in his life, and has merely been listening quite innocently on his broadcast receiving set.

What has actually happened in this case is that in tuning from one station to another he has perhaps for a minute or two to some station sending Morse, and of course, Morse had come out of Mr X's loud speaker. This has perhaps been heard through an open window or a thin wall and the enthusiastic informer immediately sends in a report accusing Mr X of illicit transmission.

57. On the other hand, it must not be assumed that because an individual does not possess transmitting apparatus he, or she can automatically be entirely exonerated; while it is true that such an individual could not be charged under No 8 of Defence Regulations, it does not necessarily follow that they are not using their wireless receiving set for, let us say, promoting pro-German propaganda. This must constantly be borne in mind, for while a well organised watch can make things very difficult for the person who desires to transmit information, there is nothing that can be done to prevent information reaching this country by wireless, and then, after being received on an ordinary everyday receiver, being used for improper or subversive purposes. In a suspected case of this nature all that can be done is to have the individual in question kept under close observation in order to obtain a check on activities and his associates.

58. One word of conclusion. It is hoped that what has been said will make it plain why it is so imperative to establish throughout the country a body of picked Voluntary Interceptors, or listeners. If another analogy may be permitted, this short wave transmission business is rather like a mashie shot at golf. The ball goes straight up in the air and comes down again at some distance. Our job is to try and pick up the divot.

59. As has already been said, the country is being divided into nine Regions, which correspond with the G.P.O. Regional Centres. This division has been decided on mainly an account of the existing distribution of trunk telegraph and telephone lines, upon which the question of rapidity on inter-communication depends.

60. Each Region will again be divided into a number of groups, each such group consisting of a number of Voluntary Interceptors, under the direction of a Group Commander, who will be responsible for his area, and for the organisation of individual members of his particular group.

When the organisation is complete each Group Commander will be in direct contact with the Regional Officer, appointed by the War Office, irrespective of the actual county boundaries in which the group in question happens to be situated.

Appendix 2: Worlledge letter

Memo from Col. Worlledge to the War Office expressing his strong views on how the RSS needed to be reformed to bring it onto a war footing.

Register No. *M.15.* **SECRET** Minute Sheet No. *2A.*

M.I.8. (Colonel)

GENERAL STAFF
M.I. 8
M 50/060
12 FEB 1941
DIRECTOR OF MILITARY OPERATIONS

With reference to the attached correspondence between Sir David Petrie, Lord Swinton and the D.M.I., my views are as follows:

As you have been for some long time well aware I consider that the present organisation of R.S.S. is unsound. I am responsible for the work done but I have no control over the personnel who carry that work out, other than the small military staff. We are dependent upon a part time service from the Post Office for the supply of all equipment, construction of stations and maintenence, and supply of personnel. The personnel are subject to their peace time terms of employment and the rules and regulations, both Post Office and Trades Union, which are based upon normal peace conditions. The Post Office organisation, being based upon peace conditions, is utterly unsuitable for war. The result is a state of incompetence and inefficiency which would not be tolerated for one moment in any fighting service. So long as the present organisation continues it will be impossible for R.S.S. ever to become properly efficient as an active war organisation.

It is not clear to me that anything would be gained by the transfer of R.S.S. "lock, stock and barrel" to any other branch unless that branch is in a position to re-organise R.S.S. completely on a proper military basis. In my opinion, R.S.S. should be organised as one unit, preferably a purely military unit though I would not exclude the possibility of a mixed military and civilian organisation. The essential point is that it should be one definite unit.

There is a very acute shortage of wireless operators in the country. Any re-organisation of R.S.S. should assure the retention of all the efficient operators and senior staff of the Post Office. The work is very highly specialised, a large proportion of the present Post Office staff have been employed on this work for nearly 18 months and it would be intolerable to lose their acquired experience and training. Authority should be retained by the Commanding Officer to select for transfer or seconding personnel from the Post Office now employed with R.S.S. Exact figures are not yet available but at a rough guess it seems likely that we could select possibly as many as 200 operators from the present staff of approximately 300 as suitable for continuance in the work. The Establishment of operators which is considered necessary is approximately 450. It would probably be necessary therefore to recruit a further 200-250 efficient operators if they can be found. There is only one source which can supply operators who already possess the necessary qualifications and experience in this work, namely, those civilians, ex-amateurs principally, who are now and have been for many months employed as Voluntary Interceptors by R.S.S., and who at the present time number about 1100. The vast majority of these are in reserved occupations or are over military age and in good jobs. A previous attempt to enlist these people in the Post Office for R.S.S. work failed owing to the small wages offered by the Post Office. In my opinion it would be necessary to offer £7. a week if we are to entice sufficient numbers of V.Is. to give up their present employment and join the unit. This would imply a similiar payment to such Post Office operators as we would accept. I am aware that this would cause repercussions in the 'Y' services and also among M.I.6's men employed on wireless work, but I can see no alternative if it is desired to make R.S.S. efficient. It must be remembered that the work is even more highly specialised and difficult than that of the 'Y' services.

The time of a considerable number of officials in the Engineer-in-Chief's Office of the G.P.O. is employed upon work for R.S.S. - supply of equipment, involving all contract work, store-keeping and store accounting, and testing of new equipment; construction of stations; major questions affecting training, posting and administration of personnel. I have serious complaints to make of the inefficienty and incompetency with which this work has been carried out, particularly with regard to the supply of equipment and construction of stations.

WL 37201/4848 100,000 1/40 KJL/875 Gp 698/3

[P.T. Over

3

Possibly much may be attributed to the fact that work for R.S.S. is only part of the work of these officials. In my opinion it is most undesirable that this state of affairs should be allowed to continue but an efficient substitute to do the work which should be done by this Post Office H.Q. staff must be found.

If M.I.6 are so organised as to enable the above desiderata to be given effect to forthwith, then the transfer of R.S.S. to M.I.6 would be obviously in the best interests of the country. It is observed that Sir David Petrie recommends that R.S.S. "be equipped, staffed, and run purely as an Intelligence instrument" by M.I.6. From a brief conversation with Colonel _____ yesterday I am left with some doubt as to whether M.I.6 does actually possess the necessary powers or administrative organisation to the extent which Sir David Petrie appears to believe.

That a very much closer liaison between M.I.6 and R.S.S. would be of great benefit to both is undeniable but this could be arranged in the present circumstances.

The work of R.S.S. concerns M.I.5 and M.I.6 and has little to do with purely Military Intelligence, nevertheless it may be anticipated that in the event of invasion a considerable number of illicit wireless transmitters will be dropped in the country, manned by soldiers in uniform. Again in the event of invasion, it seems probable that the resources of R.S.S. could be of direct military value. It would therefore appear that the D.M.I. would be directly concerned in this event with the efficiency of R.S.S.

It is therefore suggested that a reply could be made to Lord Swinton, if the D.M.I. approves, to the effect that while there does not appear to be any particular objection to the proposed transfer, it is not quite apparent what advantage is to be gained and that further information and definite proposals should be submitted for consideration.

I would like to add that Sir David Petrie's letter appears to have been written without a full knowledge of the facts. He has never spoken to me, nor has he consulted Sir Noel Ashbridge or Mr. Kirke, who were recently appointed by Lord Swinton to look into the present organisation of R.S.S. He appears to have consulted [   ] but I may say that the latter has equally small knowledge of either the technical equipment or the work done by R.S.S., his visit yesterday being the first he has paid to the unit and it was obvious from his conversation yesterday that his knowledge was very incomplete. It would appear that very much more serious consideration should be given to this proposal than appears to have been given to it up to date. The proposal is a very new one and I am seriously handicapped in expressing the opinion asked for, by my almost complete ignorance of how M.I.6 is organised and what facilities it can offer as regards the administration of both personnel and equipment. I am extremely anxious to make R.S.S. an efficient unit, but I can see no hopes of being able to do this under the present organisation. If M.I.6 can offer a solution to the difficulty I would welcome the transfer.

R.S.S.
11ᵗʰ Feb. 1941
JFGW/CEW

Colonel
Controller, Radio Security Section

DELETIONS RETAINED
UNDER SECTION 3(4)

Appendix3: Arthur Irwin's autograph book

In the course of my research I was kindly given access to an autograph book by George Brown, a radio amateur who had been friends with the late Arthur Irwin. The book had belonged to Arthur and contained sixty-five QSL cards of amateurs who had been recruited full-time into the work of the Radio Security Service. What follows are a few samples of the contents of the autograph book followed by a list of those people whose names are recorded in Arthur's book.
I have recorded their names, their radio amateur call signs, their home address as given on the cards filling out missing details where possible from Jack Hum's call book from the 1920s which listed known radio amateurs at the time. I have also recorded the date the card was written as well as any reference to where they may have met Arthur, example Barnet where Arthur and others would have completed their full time training and induction into the RSS. The majority of the QSL cards would have been given to Arthur whilst he and the owner of the QSL card were serving as Station No 4 Gilnahirk.

George Brown with Arthur's autograph book.

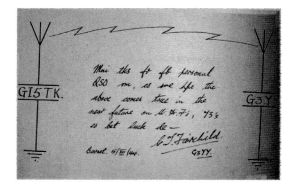

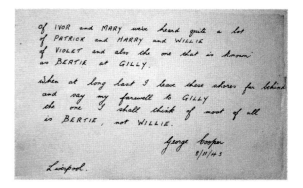

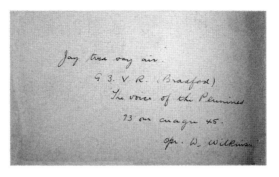

LAMENT OF A G.S. OP.

It is my lot, both day and night
To bus uphill, To heave
To toil, To search, To sweat & sweat
To lift the curves, Bank Seven.

For more long hours on murky nights
I search and search the heaven
Each suspect up, Each suspect found
Lifts up the curve, Bank Seven.

But my delight, will be the night
When I forget Bank Seven
and back to Banks & Brass return
and home, which is my Heaven.

J. Macpland. Bank Seven.
7/11/43.
OBAN ARGYLL

Jay trea vay air.
G 3. V. R. (Bradford)
The voice of the Pennines
73 ou cuagu 45.
Op. W. Wilkinson.

Portrait of a G.S. OP. at Changener

Tired was he, and worn and weary,
Like the old man in the story
Who had staggered many furlongs
With the weight of all the nations
Resting on his bending shoulders.

Tired was he but watching, anxious
Lest the signal should escape him
And be lost to Gilly's O.S.

Upward must our curve be bending
Upward! Upward sighed the Corporal
Keep it upward spoke the Major
(Very firm and very warlike)

Thus our weary listener struggled
Struggled hard to please the Corporal
Struggled to placate the Major
Did his best to get that signal
And the message that it carried.

When the job was safely copied
Handed to his Teler brother
He laid down his phones & pencil
Walked & bussed to well earned slumber
and to dreams of curves and figures.
R. Bergh. 29/10/43.

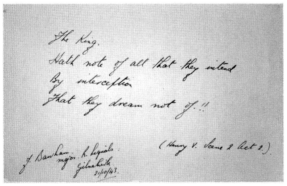

The King.
Hath note of all that they intend
By interception
That they dream not of."

(Henry V. Scene 2 Act 2.)

J. Banham. Major. R. Signals.
Gibraltar.
21/10/43.

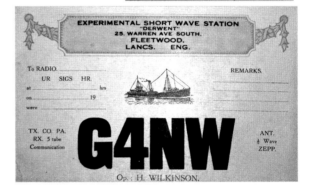

EXPERIMENTAL SHORT WAVE STATION
"DERWENT"
25. WARREN AVE SOUTH.
FLEETWOOD.
LANCS.   ENG.

To RADIO.
UR SIGS HR.
at _____ hrs
on _____ 19
were _____

REMARKS.

TX. CO. PA.
RX. 5 tube
Communication

G4NW

ANT.
½ Wave
ZEPP.

Op.: H. WILKINSON.

ENGLAND

G6LC

VPRS
WAC

One of the Old Timers
Vintage 1927

QRA:
70 Newton Road
Lowton St Marys
WARRINGTON Lancs
G6MN PRINT

To RADIO G I 5 TK.   BST
Confirming our Qso on 10/1/44 at   GMT
Your Fone/cw sigs were RST _____ on _____ Mc/s
Rx: H R O³⁵   Tx: NON EXISTANT.

MEMORIES OF GILLIE,
AND CALIBRATION.   Ant: P.O. TRIATICS
√ DIAPHRAGMS.   WITH ALL IMPEDANCE
                              FEEDERS.

PSE/TNX QSL   STANLEY INCE

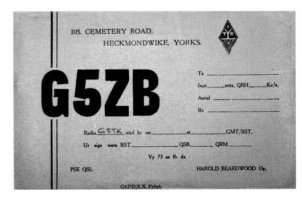

105. CEMETERY ROAD.
HECKMONDWIKE. YORKS.

G5ZB

Tx _____
Inpt ___wtts. QRH ____ Kc/s.
Aerial _____
Rx _____

Radio G 5 TK wkd hr on _____ at _____ GMT/BST,
Ur sigs were RST _____ QSB _____ QRM _____
Vy 73 es fb dx

PSE QSL   HAROLD BEARDWOOD Op.

G6PD/LX Print

141

J Stewart Owen, Clarence Road, Llandudno. 30 September 1942. G3QN. The box somewhere in England.

G H Ramsden, London, W2. 3 August 1943, G6BR, At Gilly.

J Banham, Major Royal Signals, Gilnahirk, 21 October 1943.

? Mecke, Cpl, No address, 28 October 1943. Gilnahirk.

J W Laughlin, CSM. 28 October 1943, Gilnahirk Radio Station.

J G McDowell, Sgt No address. 28 October 1943.

Lu Bright, 29 October 1943.

R Cowden, No address. 30 October 1943.

R Ussher Cree, No address. 1 November 1943.

J C Macphail, Oban, Argyll. 7 November 1943.

George Cooper, Liverpool, 8 November 1943.

Bob Loote, 17 November 1943.

J H Faulkner, No address. 17 November 1943.

J D McDonald, Thurso, Scotland. 23 November 1943.

S Ince, (Stan) St. Mary's, Warrington. 14 February 1944. G6LC. Gilnahirk.

Bob Gilchrist, Scotland, 14 March 1944.

Sydney J Briggs, Rochdale, Lancashire. (2FWZ) April 1944.

L H Baker, No address, 28 April 1944. At station No 4.

A Pritchard Sgt 29 April 1944.

F J McCormack, No address, 5 May 1944.

Cyril Hartley, Liverpool, 24 May 1944.

N A Deeble, No address, 5 June 1944. At Gilly.

Peter Dobson, No address. Concentrator Operator Gilnahirk, 5 June 1944.

H Beardwood, 105 Cemetery Road, Heckmondwike, Yorkshire. 10 June 1943, G5ZB.

F S Robinson, 15 June 1944.

R L Varney, Gallywood Road, Chelmsford. July 1944, G5RV. Gilnahirk.

Stan Wilkinson, 18 happy months spent at Gilly. 2 July 1944.

J G French, No address, 25 October 1944.

J A Clarke, 26 October 1944.

W K Miller, 37 Bee Fold Lane, Atherton, Lancashire. 11 November 1944, G6 QF. At Gilnahirk.

Adam M Little, 29 Tweed Road, Galashiels. 20 November 1944.

C Cathcart, 20 November 1944.

R S Beddie, 20 November 1944.

J Niccol, North Shields, Northhumberland. 7 December 1944.

W F Mudford, Albany Road, Blackwood. (G6BK) 12 December 1944.

C T Fairchild, 44 Hawkhurst Road, Brighton. 15 December 1944, G3YY, Met at Barnet.

A J Matthews, 74 Hawthorn Road, London, 15 December 1944, G6QM.

J R Adams, Hamilton, Scotland, 15 December 1944. G5KF.

R Smith, Box 25. 16 December 1944.

S Tollermon, Barnet, 16 December 1944.

J V Parsons, 24 Upper Holland Road, Sutton Coldfield, 16 December 1944. G5QP.

Jack Miller, Loughborough, Leics. 16 December 1944. G4MM, At Barnet.

H L Wise, St. Leonards, Sussex. 16 December 1944. G6XF.

G W Parkes, 14 Bilford Road, Worcester, 17 December 1944. G3NL. At Box 25.

A S Clacy, 8 Hangleton Road, Hove, 17 December 1944. G6CY.

J Stewart Owen, Clarence Road, Llandudno.
17 December 1944. G3QN.

L Drake ?, No address, 18 December 1944.

T Woodcock, Flamborough, Yorkshire. G6OO
18 December 1944 at PO Box 25.

G Taylor, No address, (2AGX). 18 December 1944.

R R Smith (Bob) Woodlands Road,
Gillingham. 18 December 1944.

J C Imrie, Markinch, Fife. G4GK, 18 December 1944. At Box 25.

Peter Modridge, Huton, Liverpool. 25 December 1944. G6PM.

L/Cpl, C W Homes DSM, No address given, At Gilnahirk 1944.

W Wilkinson, 10 Swainhouse Road, Bradford. No date, G3VR.

Norman H Sedgwick, Hanslope, Bletchley. No date. G8WV.

J Khikle, Caernarvonshire, N. Wales.

John McMillen, No address, No date.

Harold Wilkinson, 25 Warren Avenue South,
Fleetwood, Lancs. No dated, G4NW.

G.H. Woolner, 35 New Road, London N22. G4BC. No date.

D Williams, Swansea, South Wales. No date.

E H Staves, 19 Dunton Road, Romford, Essex. No date.

F Hooson, 25 Moreland Way, N Chingford.
G3YF, The hut at Barnet. No date.

C A Bradbury, BRS 1066. Met in London & Belfast. No date.

C R Ponting, 11 Woolcot Street, Redland,
Bristol. G6ZR. No date.

C Lingard, Alasdair, Chester Road, Cheshire,
G3IR. Met at Gilly. No date.

Dear Reader,

I hope you have enjoyed this publication from Ballyhay Books, an imprint of Laurel Cottage Ltd. We publish an eclectic mix of books ranging from personal memoirs to authoritative books on local history, from sport to poultry, from photographs to fiction and from music to marine interests – but all with a distinctly local flavour.

To see details of these books, as well as the beautifully illustrated books of our sister imprint Cottage Publications, why not visit our website **www.cottage-publications.com** or contact us on +44 (0)28 9188 8033.

Timothy S Johnston

BALLYHAY BOOKS